LANGUAGE ARTS
SKILLS & STRATEGIES

LEVEL
4

LANGUAGE ARTS
SKILLS & STRATEGIES

LEVEL **3**
LEVEL **4** ⇐
LEVEL **5**
LEVEL **6**
LEVEL **7**
LEVEL **8**

Production: Pearl Production
Cover Design: I.Q. Design, Inc.

SADDLEBACK
PUBLISHING·INC.
Three Watson
Irvine, CA 92618-2767

Website: www.sdlback.com

ISBN 1-56254-838-7

Printed in the United States of America
10 09 08 07 06 05   9 8 7 6 5 4 3 2 1

CONTENTS

CONTENTS

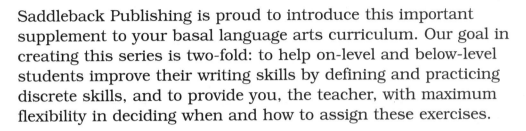

Welcome to
LANGUAGE ARTS SKILLS & STRATEGIES

Saddleback Publishing is proud to introduce this important supplement to your basal language arts curriculum. Our goal in creating this series is two-fold: to help on-level and below-level students improve their writing skills by defining and practicing discrete skills, and to provide you, the teacher, with maximum flexibility in deciding when and how to assign these exercises.

All lessons are reproducible. That makes them ideal for homework, extra credit assignments, cooperative learning groups, or focused drill practice for selected ELL or remedial students. A quick scan of the book's Table of Contents will enable you to individualize instruction according to the varied needs of your students.

Correlated to the latest research and current language arts standards in most states, the instructional design of *Language Arts Skills & Strategies* is unusually comprehensive for a supplementary program. All grade-appropriate grammar, mechanics, and usage skills are thoroughly presented from the ground up.

Assessment and evaluation of student understanding and ability is an ongoing process. A variety of methods and strategies should be used to ensure that the student is being assessed and evaluated in a fair and comprehensive manner. Here again, reproducible lessons are ideal in that they can be used for both pre- and post-testing. Always keep in mind that the assessment should take into consideration the opportunities the student had to learn the information and practice the skills presented. The strategies for assessment are left for you to determine and are dependent on your students and your particular instructional plan. The Table of Contents lists the activity by skill and can be used to assist you as you develop your assessment plan.

Remember that people's names should always begin with a capital letter.

Directions: Rewrite these names correctly on the lines below.

1. jesse owens _____

2. lisa lewis _____

3. david chung _____

4. maria lopez _____

5. eric wilson _____

Directions: Rewrite each sentence, adding capital letters where needed.

6. I saw jerry and linda at the mall.

_____

7. We met the new neighbors, lucinda and andre baxter.

_____

8. Send this letter to christa fleming.

_____

9. bryan got an email from casey fletcher.

_____

10. The coach chose amy solomon and shaun ryder as team captains.

_____

Name: _____   **Date:** _____

Remember to capitalize titles that are used as part of a person's name. You should also capitalize family titles that are used as names or as part of a person's name. And don't forget to put a period after titles that are abbreviated.

Here are a few examples:

Miss Shavers	President Lincoln
Grandpa	Lt. Skylark
Uncle Henry	Dr. Marta Hernandez

Directions: Rewrite these names correctly on the lines below.

1. mr mackey _____

2. dr sanderson _____

3. governor hawkins _____

4. miss lanier _____

5. aunt marion _____

Directions: Rewrite each sentence correctly, adding capital letters and periods where needed.

6. It was raining, so ms. smith drove us to school.

_____

7. This hallway leads to dr mack's office.

_____

8. Hayden read an exciting book about president eisenhower.

_____

9. Is this grandma's umbrella?

_____

10. mr geller used to play pro football with uncle juán.

_____

Name: _____ **Date:** _____

Always capitalize the names of pets.

Directions: Rewrite the names using capitals.

max _____   pepper _____

lady _____   buddy _____

bear _____   brandy _____

smokey _____   ginger _____

shadow _____   missy _____

Directions: These pets need names. For each pet, think of a name or choose a name from the list above. Write the pet's name on the line.

_____   _____

_____   _____

Name: _____   **Date:** _____

Capitalize the names of streets, cities, states, and countries.

Here are a few examples:
> street: Forest Hill Drive
> city: Houston
> state: Kentucky
> country: Germany

Directions: Rewrite each place name correctly.

1. london, england _____

2. hollywood, california _____

3. oakland avenue _____

4. japan _____

5. herrin, illinois _____

Directions: Answer each question with a place name.

6. What state do you live in? _____

7. What is the name of a busy street in your town? _____

8. What country would you like to visit? _____

9. What street is your school on? _____

10. What is the smallest state in the United States? _____

Name: _____   **Date:** _____

Always capitalize the names of buildings, parks, mountains, and bodies of water.

Here are a few examples:

The Museum of Modern Art   Yellowstone National Forest
Mount Everest   the Atlantic Ocean   the Black River

Directions: Rewrite each place name correctly.

1. glacier national park _____

2. the sears tower _____

3. the mississippi river _____

4. the astrodome _____

5. pike's peak _____

Directions: Underline the words that should be capitalized in each sentence.

6. I would like to visit the museum of science.

7. One of the oldest baseball fields is wrigley
   field in chicago.

8. The colorado river flows through austin,
   texas.

9. The alps are tall mountains in france.

10. This postcard shows lake ontario.

BONUS: Think of a place that you would like to visit. Write a sentence telling where
   you would like to visit and why.

_____

_____

Name: _____   **Date:** _____

Directions: Rewrite the days and months correctly.

1. The wedding will take place on saturday, june 29.

   _____

2. Does vacation begin on december 19?

   _____

3. The last day of school is thursday, may 27.

   _____

4. My grandfather was born on april 17, 1935.

   _____

5. It rained all day monday and tuesday.

   _____

Directions: Complete the sentences by writing a day or month on each line.

6. My birthday is in the month of _____.

7. We go to school from _____ until _____
   every week.

8. _____ is the first month of
   the year.

9. _____ is the last month of
   the year.

10. _____ is my favorite day of
    the week.

BONUS: Write a rhyme using at least 4 days or months.

_____

_____

Name: _____   **Date:** _____

Remember to capitalize the names of special days and holidays.

Here are a few examples:

Thanksgiving   Father's Day   Fourth of July

Directions: Read each sentence. Rewrite the holiday on the line.

1. On memorial day my family went to a parade. _____

2. I tricked my friend on april fool's day. _____

3. Joshua was born on groundhog day. _____

4. The banks were closed for columbus day. _____

5. Many people celebrate earth day. _____

6. My family celebrates kwanza. _____

7. labor day marks the end of summer. _____

8. grandparents' day isn't as well known as mother's day. _____

9. Dad gave Mom a red rose on valentine's day. _____

10. easter and passover occur around the same time of year. _____
_____

BONUS: Write a sentence about your favorite holiday.

_____

_____

Name: _____   **Date:** _____

Capitalize the names of things such as languages, religions, nationalities, businesses, organizations, schools, and teams.

Here are a few examples:

> The Oakland Raiders   Handy Hardware   French, English, Spanish

Directions: Rewrite the following names.

1. the dallas cowboys _____

2. glendale drama club _____

3. winkler school _____

4. the red cross _____

5. freshplus grocery store _____

Directions: Underline the words that should be capitalized. Then write them correctly on the lines.

6. I get my hair cut at dazzle hair salon.

_____

7. Nita speaks spanish and english.

_____

8. My friend Indira goes to a hindu temple.

_____

9. My favorite football team is the green bay packers.

_____

10. Harry gives money to the american cancer society.

_____

BONUS: Write a sentence about your favorite team or organization.

_____

_____

Name: _____   **Date:** _____

Capitalize the first word, the last word, and all the main words in the title of a book, magazine, newspaper, or movie. Do not capitalize small words, such as *for, the, in, a,* and *an,* unless they are the first or last word of the title.

In print, titles are in *italics.* You cannot write in italics, so underline titles when you write.

My teacher is reading James and the Giant Peach to us.

Directions: Capitalize and underline the following titles.

1. national velvet _____

2. highlights _____

3. the harrisburg herald _____

4. national geographic _____

5. the wizard of oz _____

Directions: Write each sentence correctly. Underline and capitalize the titles.

6. The movie seabiscuit is based on a true story.

_____

7. Jackie reads the seattle sentinel every morning.

_____

8. Have you read ali baba and the forty thieves?

_____

9. my baby brother's favorite book is pat the bunny.

_____

10. Maya reads critters magazine every month.

_____

Name: _____   **Date:** _____

Use a capital letter to show where a sentence begins. Use end punctuation to show where it ends.

Here's an example:
the beach was quiet the water lapped softly on the soft sand
The beach was quiet. The water lapped softly on the soft sand.

Directions: Add capital letters and end punctuation to the following groups of words. Some groups should be divided into two sentences. Write them on the lines.

1. lawrence hopped out of the car

_____

2. the wind mussed his hair he ran to the water's edge

_____

3. mom and aunt kathy followed with the picnic basket

_____

4. lawrence let the water lap at his toes it was chilly

_____

5. mom called to him he ran to help carry the folding chairs

_____

6. aunt kathy opened the big beach umbrella she stuck it in the sand

_____

7. lawrence helped mom spread out the big blanket

_____

8. then they all splashed into the water

_____

9. they had a wonderful time at the beach

_____

Name: _____ **Date:** _____

A friendly letter consists of six parts: inside address, date, greeting, body, closing, and signature. The greeting and closing should be capitalized.

Directions: Ian wrote a letter to his aunt. He forgot to use capitals. Circle all the letters that should be capitalized.

3622 burnet drive
freeport, california 92109
august 12, 2003

dear aunt carol,

thank you so very much for the beautiful card. i put it on my dresser. now i can look at it every day.

the summer seems to be flying by quickly. monica and i have been busy the whole time. we both went to basketball camp for two weeks. we also took an art class at the freeport school of art. both were lots of fun! please visit us soon. we miss you.

love,

ian

Directions: Rewrite the sentences. Use capital letters where needed.

1. lorenzo went to madrid to visit his uncle felipe last july.

   _____

2. it was his first trip to spain.

   _____

3. the airplane crossed the atlantic ocean.

   _____

4. uncle felipe had many activities planned.

   _____

5. he took lorenzo to the prado, a famous museum.

   _____

6. there were several paintings by pablo picasso.

   _____

7. later, they went to a movie theater to see toy story in spanish.

   _____

8. lorenzo liked playing with uncle felipe's dog rosita.

   _____

9. after two weeks, it was time to fly back to minnesota.

   _____

10. next thanksgiving, uncle felipe will come to visit.

    _____

BONUS: Write two sentences telling a friend or uncle what plans
you have for their upcoming visit.

_____

_____

Name: _____   **Date:** _____

Periods, question marks, and exclamation points are end marks.
They show where a sentence ends.
  • Use a period at the end of a statement.
  • Use a question mark at the end of a question.

Here are two examples:

> Mark likes science.
> Has he been to the science museum?

Directions: Complete each sentence by adding a period or a question mark.

1. The bus will pick us up after the game_____

2. Who is playing tonight_____

3. Dad has always rooted for the Vikings_____

4. Mom is a Giants fan_____

5. Is it snowing now_____

6. Mom packed blankets for us_____

7. Did you bring your gloves and hat_____

8. It will be chilly during the game_____

9. Let's take some hot chocolate with us_____

10. Do you want marshmallows in it_____

BONUS: Write two sentences about a sporting event.

_____

_____

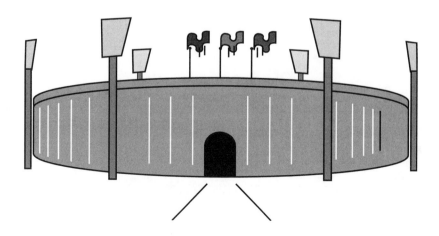

Name: _____   **Date:** _____

Remember that an exclamation is a sentence that shows a strong feeling. It ends with an exclamation point.

Directions: Complete each sentence by adding a period or an exclamation point.

1. This sandwich is huge_____

2. I will save half of it for later_____

3. Oh no, my glasses fell in the pool_____

4. Art class was so fun today_____

5. The plates are in the cupboard_____

6. I loved that book_____

7. Tony will be home at 7:00_____

8. What a beautiful song_____

9. I think this plant needs some water_____

10. Your brother is really funny_____

11. He is always telling jokes on the bus_____

12. The one about the pigs was awesome_____

13. I wonder who told him that joke_____

14. What I would give to be funny_____

15. I have a hard time remembering jokes_____

BONUS: Suppose someone just told you something very exciting. Write a few sentences telling what that person said and what your said in response.

_____

_____

_____

_____

Name: _____   **Date:** _____

Directions: Read each sentence. Decide whether each is a statement, a question, or an exclamation. Write the correct punctuation mark on the line.

1. Dave and I are best friends_____

2. Did you know that we have the same birthday_____

3. That is so strange_____

4. Last year we had a birthday party together_____

5. Our parents took us to Water World_____

6. Have you ever been there_____

7. The Captain was my favorite giant slide_____

8. It's huge_____

9. Do you like to go fast_____

10. If you do, you will love The Captain_____

11. Dave likes the log ride the best_____

12. My sister couldn't ride on it last year_____

13. How old is your sister_____

14. You have to be five to go on the log ride_____

15. I can't wait to go back to Water World_____

Name: _____   **Date:** _____

Possessive nouns show that someone or something has or owns something. If the noun is plural, add –'s to show ownership. If the noun is plural and ends in –s, add –'.

Singular	Plural
Carl's team	the boys' team
Alison's sister	the dogs' trainer
the book's title	the students' teacher

If a plural noun does not end in –s, add –'s to show ownership.

the children's mother

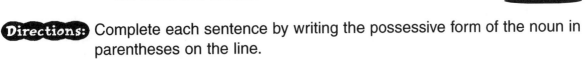

Directions: Complete each sentence by writing the possessive form of the noun in parentheses on the line.

1. (Oscar) We are going to _____ house.

2. (sheep) The _____ wool needed to be cut.

3. (candle) This _____ odor is too strong.

4. (computer) My _____ screen is too small.

5. (horses) The woman braided the _____ tails.

6. (Farley) Will _____ friend come with us?

7. (oxen) The _____ feet sank deep into the mud.

8. (plant) This _____ leaves are velvety.

9. (Dr. Seuss) Many children love _____ books.

10. (men) Where is the _____ department in this store?

Name: _____   Date: _____

Language Arts Skills & Strategies, Level 4 • Saddleback Publishing, Inc. ©2005 • 3 Watson, Irvine, CA 92618 • Phone (888) 735-2225 • www.sdlback.com   21

The word *won't* is a special contraction for *will + not*. The word *can't* is a short form of the word *cannot*.

A contraction is a word made from two words joined together and shortened. An apostrophe takes the place of the letters that are taken out of the words. In the contraction *don't,* the apostrophe takes the place of the letter *o.*

EXAMPLES:

is not	isn't	do not	don't
are not	aren't	does not	doesn't
was not	wasn't	did not	didn't
were not	weren't	could not	couldn't
has not	hasn't	should not	shouldn't
have not	haven't	would not	wouldn't
had not	hadn't	cannot	can't

Directions: Write the words that make up the following contractions.

1. wasn't _____

2. don't _____

3. couldn't _____

4. shouldn't _____

5. hadn't _____

Directions: Write contractions for the following words.

6. has not _____

7. would not _____

8. are not _____

9. will not _____

10. is not _____

Name: _____   **Date:** _____

Notice that –'s can stand for *is* or *has* in the contractions *it's*, *he's*, and *she's*.

You can form contractions with pronouns and some verbs. Use an apostrophe to show where letters were taken out.

I am	I'm	it will	it'll
he is	he's	we will	we'll
she is	she's	they will	they'll
it is	it's	he has	he's
you are	you're	she has	she's
we are	we're	it has	it's
they are	they're	I have	I've
I will	I'll	you have	you've
you will	you'll	we have	we've
he will	he'll	they have	they've
she will	she'll		

Directions: Write contractions for the underlined words.

1. <u>She is</u> going to love how her room looks.

   _____

2. <u>It is</u> a surprise. _____

3. <u>They have</u> chosen a great color for the walls.

   _____

4. <u>It will</u> take a long time for the paint to dry.

   _____

5. <u>You have</u> smeared the paint! _____

6. <u>He has</u> fixed it already. _____

7. <u>We are</u> going to hang up curtains. _____

8. <u>They are</u> blue and yellow. _____

9. <u>They have</u> got a matching rug. _____

10. <u>It will</u> look great with the blue walls. _____

Name: _____   **Date:** _____

A series is a list of three or more words or groups of words in a sentence. Use commas to separate items in a series. Use the word *and* or *or* before the last item in the series.

Here are two examples:

We need <u>paper</u>, <u>scissors</u>, <u>glue</u>, and <u>markers</u> for this project.
We will <u>cut shapes</u>, <u>color them</u>, and <u>glue them together</u>.

Directions: Add commas to the following sentences.

1. My hobbies are reading drawing and playing basketball.

2. The new uniforms are blue white and green.

3. We wear long pants white shirts and blue ties.

4. Mickey Robert Julie and Ashley worked on their project.

5. Playing tag jumping rope and dancing are fun ways to exercise.

Directions: Write sentences using the series of words below. Remember to include commas and a connecting word such *as* and or *or*.

6. tiger, lion, panther, jaguar

_____

7. flour, eggs, milk

_____

8. Jenny, Matt, Frank, Thomas

_____

9. car, truck, boat, plane

_____

10. go fishing, hike in the woods, swim in the lake

_____

Name: _____   **Date:** _____

Commas show where to pause in a sentence. Use a comma after the words *yes, no,* and *well* when they begin a sentence. Use a comma after order words when they begin a sentence. Some order words are *first, second, next,* and *finally.*

      EXAMPLE: Well, how was the movie?

Use commas to set off the name of someone who is being addressed, or spoken to, directly.

      EXAMPLE: We hope, David, that you'll stay here with us.

Directions: Read the sentences below. Add commas where they are needed.

1. Greg have you read this new book?

2. Yes I read it last week Simon.

3. Well did you like it?

4. Yes it was interesting.

5. What is it about Greg?

6. Well it is somewhat hard to explain.

7. You'll have to read it for yourself Simon.

Directions: Answer each question with a sentence beginning with *yes, no, well,* or an order word. Write your answers on the lines.

8. Have you ever seen an elephant?

   _____

   _____

9. What is the first thing you do every morning?

   _____

   _____

10. Do you like pickles?

   _____

   _____

Name: _____   **Date:** _____

When two short sentences have ideas that go together, you can combine them to make one sentence. Use a comma and the word *and, but,* or *or* to combine them. *And, but,* and *or* are called connecting words.

EXAMPLE: We gave the dog a bath. He still smells like skunk.
We gave the dog a bath, but he still smells like skunk.

Directions: Combine each pair of sentences to form one sentence. Use a comma and the connecting word in parentheses.

1. The Clarkville Zoo is small. It is interesting. (but)

_____

2. The zoo takes care of animals that nobody wants. They have a good life at the zoo. (and)

_____

3. The animals were rescued from bad situations. They were given away by their owners. (or)

_____

4. Some of the monkeys and parrots were once pets. The owners could not take care of them. (but)

_____

5. The lion used to be in a circus. The tiger was kept in a tiny cage by its owner. (and)

_____

6. Exotic animals are beautiful. They do not make good pets. (but)

_____

7. You can enter free. It is good to give a donation. (but)

_____

8. You can donate money. You can donate supplies. (or)

_____

9. Many of the animals love fruit. They eat lots of vegetables. (and)

_____

10. I took a bag of apples once. The zoo keepers were happy to take them. (and)

_____

Name: _____ **Date:** _____

Remember to use commas to separate the day and the year when writing dates.

EXAMPLE: February 2, 2007

Directions: Add commas to the following dates.

1. March 4 1966

2. April 17 1935

3. December 12 2003

4. February 21 1844

5. July 1 2001

6. January 17 1999

7. September 8 2005

8. November 15 1987

9. June 24 1866

10. October 10 1785

BONUS: Think about three important dates in your life. On the lines below, write a sentence about each, telling why it is important.

_____

_____

_____

_____

_____

_____

Name: _____   **Date:** _____

Use commas to separate the city and state when writing addresses. Also use a comma to separate a city and its country.

Here are two examples:

Henderson, Georgia   Caracas, Venezuela

Directions: Add commas to the following addresses.

1. 4072 Gleane St.
   Elmhurst NY 11373

2. 4754 Francisco Dr.
   Pensacola FL 32504

3. 862 Illinois Ave.
   Chicago IL 60609

4. 29 Compo Road
   Westport CT 06880

5. 1224 Bob Herman Rd.
   Atlanta GA 31408

Directions: Read each sentence and add commas where needed.

6. The acropolis is in Athens Greece.

7. Jan's pen pal lives in Casablanca Morocco.

8. George's grandparents came from Monterrey Mexico.

9. Reykjavik Iceland is a chilly place to live.

10. Have you ever heard of Bydgoszcz Poland?

Name: _____   **Date:** _____

Directions: Read the sentences and add commas where needed.

1. Gina Shannon and Courtney wrote a play together.

2. I read it and it is pretty good.

3. Holly won't be old enough to vote until May 15 2015.

4. Alexandria Egypt is an ancient city.

5. Yes Josh you can have a snack.

6. First go wash your hands.

7. I will slice an apple for you or you can eat a banana.

8. The students wrote reports made posters and gave speeches about air pollution.

9. Tomorrow Mr. Hawkins I will come on time.

10. Mr. Hawkins gave us instructions for the project.

11. First we must gather the materials.

12. We will need posters paper markers scissors and glue.

13. We use the markers to draw decorate and number each shape.

14. Next we need to cut out the shapes and glue them on the poster.

15. Finally we need to let the glue dry for several hours.

BONUS: Write two sentences that include a series or the name of a city and a country. Make sure to place the commas where you need them.

_____

_____

_____

Name: _____   **Date:** _____

An abbreviation is a shortened form of a word. Most abbreviations begin with a capital letter and end with a period. The names of days and months are often written as abbreviations. Notice that *May, June,* and *July* do not have abbreviated forms.

DAYS OF THE WEEK

Sunday	Sun.
Monday	Mon.
Tuesday	Tues.
Wednesday	Wed.
Thursday	Thurs.
Friday	Fri.
Saturday	Sat.

MONTHS

January	Jan.	July	—
February	Feb.	August	Aug.
March	Mar.	September	Sept.
April	Apr.	October	Oct.
May	—	November	Nov.
June	—	December	Dec.

Directions: Write each abbreviation correctly.

1. nov _____

2. tues _____

3. dec _____

4. thurs _____

5. apr _____

Directions: Write the correct abbreviation for each day and month.

6. Wednesday _____

7. October _____

8. Monday _____

9. February _____

10. Sunday _____

Name: _____   **Date:** _____

Some titles and certain words used in addresses are often abbreviated. Most begin with a capital letter and end with a period.

Remember, "Miss" is not an abbreviation and does not end with a period.

TITLES		ADDRESSES	
Mister	Mr.	Street	St.
a married woman	Mrs.	Road	Rd.
any woman	Ms.	Avenue	Ave.
Doctor	Dr.	Boulevard	Blvd.
Junior	Jr.	Company	Co.
Senior	Sr.	Post Office	P. O.

Directions: Write each name correctly.

1. ms rosen _____

2. dr thomas _____

3. allen hastings, sr _____

4. miss elliot _____

5. mrs haverty _____

Directions: Rewrite each address, replacing each underlined word with an abbreviation.

6. <u>Doctor</u> Alysha Kenner _____

   342 Poston <u>Road</u> _____

7. Earl Vallery, <u>Junior</u> _____

   856 Henley <u>Boulevard</u> _____

8. <u>Mister</u> Salem Al Hassan _____

   785 Baxter <u>Avenue</u> _____

9. Olson Coffee <u>Company</u> _____

   <u>Post Office</u> Box 4550 _____

10. Jerry Paxton, <u>Senior</u> _____

    6743 College <u>Street</u> _____

Name: _____   **Date:** _____

When you write the exact words that someone says, you are writing a direct quotation. Always put quotation marks at the beginning and end of the person's exact words.

Here is an example:

"I hid the diamonds under the sofa," she whispered in his ear.

Directions: Add quotation marks to the sentences below.

1. Victor asked, Where are my keys?

2. You are always late! Cody complained

3. I'll be there, assured Sam

4. Marie cried, Look out for that swarm of bees!

5. I'll see you in six months, said the hygienist.

6. I'll never tell your secret, she promised.

7. Your voice is so loud! scolded Ms. Jones.

8. Give me liberty or give me death, declared Patrick Henry.

9. Dave lost my book! moaned Todd.

10. Put things back where you found them, instructed my teacher.

Name: _____   **Date:** _____

When a direct quotation comes at the end of a sentence, use a comma before the first quotation marks. Begin the direct quotation with a capital letter. Put the end mark inside the last quotation marks.

Here is an example:
Warren yelled, "Don't touch my clean car with those dirty hands!"

Directions: Each sentence contains a direct quotation. Add commas, capital letters, and quotation marks.

1. The teacher asked who knows this story?

   _____

2. Lisa cried that's one of my favorites!

   _____

3. Ethan sighed it always rains on Saturday.

   _____

4. Mr. Morton called who wants to go for a drive?

   _____

5. Andre wondered how do they change the bulbs on radio towers?

   _____

6. Mom shouted get in here right now, Montel!

   _____

7. Kimberly replied no, that's not my hat.

   _____

8. Gordon exclaimed now I've seen it all!

   _____

9. Nellie whispered you're stepping on my foot, Brandon.

   _____

10. Anson suggested wash it and put a bandage on it.

   _____

Name: _____   **Date:** _____

The rules are different when a direct quotation comes at the beginning of a sentence. If the direct quotation is statement or a command, put a comma at the end of the direct quotation, inside the last quotation marks. If the direct quotation is an exclamation or a question, put the exclamation point or question mark inside the last quotation marks.

Always begin any quotation with a capital letter.

Statement: "I brought you some flowers," said Tony.
Command: "Pick up your toys," directed Ms. Handey.
Question: "Who ate all the raisins?" asked Jennifer.
Exclamation: "This pizza is terrific!" cried Patrick.

Directions: Each sentence contains a direct quotation. Add commas, capital letters, and quotation marks.

1. I'll drive you home now said Mrs. Johnson.

_____

2. What a huge stadium cried Matthew.

_____

3. What do bears do in the winter asked Sherman.

_____

4. They hibernate answered Jake.

_____

5. Go brush your teeth ordered Mom.

_____

6. Will you help me with my math problems asked Drew.

_____

7. Can hummingbirds really fly backwards wondered Kathryn.

_____

8. Yes, they sure can I replied.

_____

9. What a mess you've made exclaimed Tabitha.

_____

10. What color paint did you choose asked Molly.

_____

Name: _____   **Date:** _____

You have already learned to capitalize and underline the titles of books, magazines, newspapers, and movies. Other titles use quotation marks instead of underlining. Set quotation marks around the titles of songs, short stories, and poems.

Directions: Each sentence contains the title of a song, short story, or poem. Add quotation marks where needed.

1. Always and Forever was my parents' wedding song.

2. Have you ever read the short story The Boar Pig by Saki?

3. My dad's favorite poem is If by Rudyard Kipling.

4. Hetta read a poem called If I Could.

5. The crowd sang Take Me Out to the Ballgame together.

6. My little brother loves to sing Old McDonald over and over.

7. The Star Spangled Banner is often sung at sporting events.

8. Graham read a scary story called The Locked Door.

9. The short story Tiny Dancer was made into a movie.

10. Who Ordered the Broiled Face? is a silly poem by Shel Silverstein.

BONUS: Write a sentence about a song you like. Write another sentence about a song you don't like. Include the titles of the songs in the sentences.

_____

_____

_____

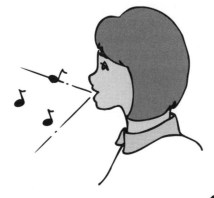

Name: _____   **Date:** _____

Parentheses can be used around extra information you want to include in a sentence. The information you enclose in parentheses is not very important to the meaning of the sentence. It should be minor enough to leave out without changing the meaning of the sentence.

Here are two examples:

All the students (there are 33) loved the play.
Grandpa Tito (my mom's father) will come to visit soon.

Directions: Read each sentence and decide which piece of extra information from the box belongs in the parentheses. Write it on the line.

EXTRA INFORMATION
---

the boys	one hour from now
on the grill	soccer and reading
I'm 8 and Grayson is 11	they moved in last week
my favorite kind	dusting and vacuuming
the ones with the red flowers	I'm a vegetarian

1. Our new neighbors _____ are coming over for dinner tonight.

2. They're going to be here at 7:00 _____.

3. Dad is busy roasting a chicken _____.

4. Mom is making a bean salad for me _____.

5. For dessert, we're having chocolate cake _____ and ice cream.

6. Grayson and I are helping by cleaning _____ the living room.

7. Next, we will set the table with the good dishes _____ _____.

8. The neighbors have two boys our age _____ _____.

9. I haven't met them _____ yet, but Grayson has.

10. Grayson says they like the same things we do _____ _____.

Directions: These sentences contain punctuation mistakes. Find them and write the sentences correctly.

1. Dr Karnes isnt at work today.

   _____

2. What did you do today.

   _____

3. Im not allergic to cats.

   _____

4. Please bring a pen some paper and a ruler to class.

   _____

5. Huckleberry Finn is my favorite book.

   _____

6. I am so happy you called! cried Aunt Donna.

   _____

7. Is this Garys backpack?

   _____

8. First we need set a date for the party.

   _____

9. Maxine was born March 28 1998 in Norman Oklahoma.

   _____

10. Jack is tall but the giant is taller.

   _____

A sentence tells a complete thought. It names a person, place, or thing and tells *what is* or *what happens.* Sentences include a noun and a verb, also known as a subject and a predicate.

Complete sentence: The bright sun hurt my eyes.

The bright sun names a person, place, or thing. *Hurt my eyes* tells what happens.

Directions: Underline the complete sentences.

Hid under the steps in the hall.

Is teasing everyone with his comments.

Are going to watch the show.

Drew thrilled the audience with her performance.

Most of the students.

The lifeguard patrolled the beach in a red jeep.

Takes a long time to cook.

I sent the invitations over a week ago.

The man with the blue jacket is my neighbor.

Took my dog for a walk.

Name: _____

Date: _____

Sentences need two parts to make a complete thought. The subject tells *who* or *what.* The predicate tells what the subject *is* or *does.*

A complete subject is made up of all the words in the subject. A complete predicate is all the words that make up the predicate. Both may be a single word or a group of words.

Complete Subject	Complete Predicate
The tiny dog	barked fiercely at the cat.
The cat	hissed.
I	like dogs.

Directions: Underline the complete subject of each sentence. Draw a circle around the complete predicate.

1. The pitcher practiced his fastball until he got it perfect.

2. The chef prepared a tasty stew.

3. Bert tripped on the rug.

4. The concerts usually last about an hour.

5. Mr. and Mrs. Trimble keep their garden tidy.

6. The huge grizzly bear yawned lazily.

7. Robin answered the phone.

8. Frankie played a joke on his little sister.

9. I enjoy playing kickball.

10. Ian's friend Barry came over.

BONUS: Write a sentence. Underline the complete subject and draw a circle around the complete predicate.

_____

_____

_____

Name: _____   **Date:** _____

A complete subject is made up of all the words in the subject. It can be one word or a group of words. The main word in a complete subject is called the **simple subject**.

EXAMPLE: The wooden **gate** was hard to push open.

In this sentence, *The wooden gate* is the complete subject. The simple subject is *gate. Gate* is the main word of the complete subject.

EXAMPLE: Max was excited about the play.

In this sentence, the complete subject and the simple subject are the same: *Max.*

Directions: Underline the simple subject in each sentence.

1. The knight was afraid of nothing.

2. All the other knights admired him.

3. He was known for his bravery.

4. The king rewarded the knight's bravery.

5. The princess married the gallant knight.

Directions: Complete each sentence by adding a complete subject to each predicate. Then draw a circle around the simple subject in each complete subject you write.

6. _____ jokes about everything.

7. _____ broke into a hundred pieces.

8. _____ ran home squealing.

9. _____ eats nothing but leaves and grass.

10. _____ sat by the fireplace reading a book.

Name: _____ **Date:** _____

The complete predicate of a sentence is the word or group of words that tells what the subject is doing or being. The main word in a complete predicate is called the **simple predicate**.

EXAMPLE: The candle <u>flickered</u> in the breeze.

In this sentence, *flickered in the breeze* is the complete predicate. The simple predicate is *flickered*.

EXAMPLE: The coyotes <u>howled</u>.

In this sentence, the complete predicate and the simple predicate are the same: *howled*.

Directions: Underline the simple predicate in each sentence.

1. Artie usually practices the piano after school.
2. The soap bubbles popped on the grass.
3. Brian drinks a liter of water before every game.
4. All of our relatives arrived late for the reunion.
5. The ice cubes melted.
6. The turtles snapped at the tiny fish.
7. That sandwich looks delicious.
8. Jan wants to play the guitar.
9. The red balloon floated up into the sky.
10. The game lasted thirty minutes.

BONUS: Write two sentences about coyotes. Circle the simple predicate in each sentence.

_____

_____

_____

_____

Name: _____   **Date:** _____

You have learned how to combine two short, related sentences with a comma and the word *and, but,* or *or.* The new sentence is called a **compound sentence**.

Here is an example:
Jennifer writes stories. Marc draws pictures for them.
Jennifer writes stories, and Marc draws pictures for them.

Directions: Combine each pair of sentences to form one compound sentence. Use a comma and the connecting word in parentheses.

1. Bill went to Justin's house. Justin wasn't home. (but)

   _____

2. The concert is free. You have to pay to park. (but)

   _____

3. The fireworks were fantastic. We wanted them to last all night. (and)

   _____

4. You fold the napkins. I'll iron the tablecloth. (and)

   _____

5. Would you like to play a game? Would you rather do a puzzle? (or)

   _____

Directions: Write a subject and predicate on the line to form a compound sentence.

6. Dana likes pizza, but _____.

7. The cat's name is Muffin, and _____.

8. You can clean your room, or _____.

9. The students opened their books, and _____.

10. I put my hands over my ears, but _____.

Name: _____ Date: _____

42 Language Arts Skills & Strategies, Level 4 • Saddleback Publishing, Inc. ©2005 • 3 Watson, Irvine, CA 92618 • Phone (888) 735-2225 • www.sdlback.com

You have learned that the main word in a complete subject is called the simple subject. A **compound subject** has two or more main words, joined by a connecting word. The subjects have the same predicate.

EXAMPLE: <u>The boy and his dog</u> walked through the park.

The compound subject here is *the boy* and *his dog.* The subjects share the predicate *walked through the park.*

Directions: Underline the sentences that have a compound subject.

1. Marshall and Marty are brothers and adventurers.

2. They have been filming wildlife for nearly twenty years.

3. Cougars and bears are interesting animals to film.

4. Marty is the main photographer.

5. He and Marshall spend hours in the forest waiting to see animals.

6. Sitting quietly and waiting patiently can be boring, says Marshall.

7. That is the only way to film animals in the wild, though.

8. My sister and I rented their videos.

9. We watched them with our parents.

10. My family and I enjoyed them all.

Name: _____   Date: _____

The main word in a complete predicate is called the simple predicate. A **compound predicate** has two or more main words, joined by a connecting word. The predicates have the same subject.

EXAMPLE: The tiny baby just <u>sleeps</u> and <u>eats</u>.

The compound predicate here is *sleeps* and *eats*. The verbs share the subject *The tiny baby*.

EXAMPLE: Sue <u>walked</u> slowly down the hall and <u>admired</u> the artwork.

In this sentence, the compound predicate is *walked* and *admired*.

Directions: Underline the sentences that have a compound predicate.

1. Henry opened the box and looked under the wrappings.
2. Lisa ran for the bus.
3. The tall tree shaded and cooled the yard.
4. Maxwell is a skilled detective.
5. San Francisco is often cool and windy in the summer.
6. Simone enjoys action movies.
7. Derek opened the refrigerator and took out the milk.
8. I adore my little brother Schuler.
9. The noisy children tooted horns and banged on drums.
10. Everyone clapped and cheered during the concert.

Name: _____

Date: _____

A noun names a person, place, or thing.

Persons	**Places**	**Things**
Alice	Dallas	shoe
baby	garden	clock
aunt	store	apples

Directions: Fill in the blanks with nouns.

1. (Person) _____ walked to the (place) _____ .

2. The (thing) _____ rang at midnight.

3. (Place) _____ is my favorite place to go in my free time.

4. This (thing) _____ belongs to (person) _____ .

5. (Person) _____ won a (thing) _____ at the fair.

Directions: Underline the nouns in the story. Write them in the table.

The restaurant was busy. The customers were lined up outside the door. They were eager to try Chef Pierre's amazing pizza. Inside, waiters scurried about, carrying trays and dishes.

"This is delicious!" cried George. He smacked his lips.

"It certainly is," replied Treena. "In fact, I think this is the best pizza in all of Rooterville," she continued. "I'm going to write an article about it in my newspaper tomorrow."

PERSONS	**PLACES**	**THINGS**

Name: _____   **Date:** _____

There are two kinds of nouns. A **common noun** is a noun that names any person, place, or thing.

A **proper noun** names a particular person, place, or thing. Proper nouns should always begin with a capital letter.

	Common	**Proper**
Person:	uncle	Uncle Stan
Place:	country	England
Thing:	horse	Seabiscuit

Directions: Write proper nouns to finish the chart. One of them has been done for you.

	COMMON—PROPER
Person	actress—_____
	singer—_____
Place	state—*Kansas*
	country—_____
Thing	book—_____
	holiday—_____

Directions: Circle the common nouns. Underline the proper nouns. Write the proper nouns correctly on the lines.

1. My cousin lives in california. _____

2. This dog's name is rufus. _____

3. The teachers at brush school are nice. _____

4. How many stars make up the big dipper? _____

5. hawaii is made up of several islands. _____

A **singular noun** names only one person, place, or thing. A **plural noun** names more than one.

one airplane	two airplanes
one van	ten vans

To form the plural, add –s to most singular nouns. If a noun ends in –ch, –x, –sh, or –s, make it plural by adding –es.

boss	bosses
tax	taxes
bush	bushes

Directions: Write the plural form of each noun.

1. box _____

2. drum _____

3. recess _____

4. brush _____

5. chair _____

6. puzzle _____

7. eyelash _____

8. peach _____

9. host _____

10. bowl _____

Directions: Find one noun in each sentence that should be plural. Write the noun correctly on the line.

11. Put all of the plate in the sink with some water. _____

12. We can fit both box in the closet in the hall. _____

13. This puppy is covered with spot. _____

14. He has a long tail and black ear. _____

15. There is room in this lunch box for three sandwich. _____

Language Arts Skills & Strategies, Level 4 • Saddleback Publishing, Inc. ©2005 • 3 Watson, Irvine, CA 92618 • Phone (888) 735-2225 • www.sdlback.com

Name: _____   **Date:** _____

There are special rules for forming the plural of nouns that end in *y*. If a noun ends with a vowel and *y*, add –*s*.

monkey	monkeys
day	days
valley	valleys

If a noun ends with a consonant and *y*, change the *y* to *i* and add –*ies*.

city	cities
berry	berries
family	families

Directions: Write the plural form of each noun.

1. lady _____

2. birthday _____

3. puppy _____

4. key _____

5. toy _____

6. ruby _____

7. hobby _____

8. fly _____

9. ferry _____

10. body _____

Directions: Complete each sentence by writing the plural form of the noun in parentheses.

11. This author writes _____ for children. (story)

12. How many _____ are in this town? (library)

13. Tom rides his bike through the _____ behind the houses. (alley)

14. Glowworms and _____ light up at night. (firefly)

15. Three angry _____ screamed at the cat. (bluejay)

Some nouns have special plural forms. Study this list. Notice the spellings of the plural forms of the nouns.

Singular	Plural
child	children
man	men
woman	women
foot	feet
tooth	teeth
goose	geese
ox	oxen
mouse	mice

Some nouns do not change at all in the plural. Their singular and plural forms are the same.

Singular	Plural
one deer	some deer
one moose	two moose
one sheep	many sheep

Directions: Complete each sentence by writing the plural form of the noun in parentheses.

1. The tiny bat had many sharp _____. (tooth)

2. Those birds flying by may be ducks or _____. (goose)

3. Three of these _____ have brown wool. (sheep)

4. A team of _____ pulled the heavy cart. (ox)

5. The two baby _____ followed their mother everywhere. (moose)

Directions: Is the underlined noun in each sentence singular or plural? Write *Singular* or *Plural* on the line.

6. Most <u>deer</u> run away at the sight of humans. _____

7. The white <u>mouse</u> had red eyes. _____

8. The <u>women</u> carried the boxes upstairs. _____

9. Wipe your <u>feet</u> on the mat before entering. _____

10. When she was a <u>child</u>, Grandma had red hair. _____

Name: _____   **Date:** _____

There are several ways to form plural nouns.

Add *–s*: kites, days, gloves

Add *–es*: brushes, benches, boxes, buses

Change *y* to *i* then add *–es*: cities, puppies

Special plurals: men, geese, oxen

No change: deer, moose, sheep

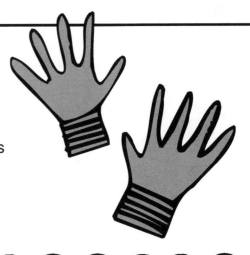

Directions: Write the plural form of each noun.

1. one company, two _____

2. one notebook, two _____

3. one batch, two _____

4. one mouse, two _____

5. one radish, two _____

6. one sheep, two _____

7. one table, two _____

8. one foot, two _____

9. one circus, two _____

10. one party, two _____

11. one child, two _____

12. one pony, two _____

13. one holiday, two _____

14. one plant, two _____

15. one fly, two _____

16. one wish, two _____

17. one daisy, two _____

18. one tulip, two _____

19. one tooth, two _____

20. one lunch, two _____

Name: _____   **Date:** _____

A possessive noun tells who or what owns or has something. A **singular possessive noun** shows ownership by one person or thing. You form the possessive of a singular noun by adding *–'s*.

I see a boy. The boy's jacket is blue.
This is Chris. Chris's mom works at our school.

Directions: Make the following nouns possessive.

1. _____ house (Brad)

2. the _____ collar (dog)

3. my _____ job (uncle)

4. a _____ phone number (friend)

5. the _____ microphone (singer)

6. _____ shoes (Tess)

7. the _____ mane (lion)

8. the _____ ticket (passenger)

9. my _____ room (sister)

10. the _____ handle (broom)

Singular possessive nouns show ownership by one person or thing. A **plural possessive noun** shows ownership by two or more persons or things.

If a plural noun ends in –s, add an apostrophe after the s to show ownership.

> two players' coach
> these workers' boss

If a noun is plural but does not end in s, add –'s to show ownership.

> the children's grandfather

Directions: Make these plural words possessive.

1. my _____ party (friends)

2. some _____ antlers (moose)

3. ten _____ barn (cows)

4. the _____ team (women)

5. most _____ rules (factories)

6. five _____ feathers (geese)

7. all the _____ wagons (pioneers)

8. many _____ suitcases (guests)

9. three _____ tails (mice)

10. two _____ armor (knights)

Name: _____ Date: _____

Rules for forming possessive nouns:

Add –'s to singular nouns: the clown's nose

Add –' to plural nouns ending in –s: two girls' teacher

Add –'s to plural nouns that do not end in –s: three children's books

Directions: Complete each sentence by writing the possessive form of the verb in parentheses.

1. My _____ names are Billie, Mack, and Ray. (friends)

2. I once found a _____ notebook. (girl)

3. I took it to the _____ office. (principal)

4. The three _____ eyes were brown. (brothers)

5. Their _____ eyes were green. (sisters)

6. The _____ illustrations made me laugh. (book)

7. The _____ ending was sad. (story)

8. All the _____ hair was black. (children)

9. This _____ seats are comfortable. (theater)

10. The _____ science project won a prize. (students)

A pronoun is a word used to take the place of one or more nouns. You can use them when writing to avoid repeating nouns again and again.

<u>Dave and Maria</u> went to a play. <u>They</u> had free tickets.

The pronoun *They* takes the place of the nouns *Dave* and *Maria.*

Like nouns, pronouns can be singular or plural. The pronoun *you* can be singular or plural.

Singular pronouns: I, me, you, he, him, she, her, it
Plural pronouns: we, us, you, they, them

Directions: Read each pair of sentences. Circle the pronoun in the second sentence. Underline the word or words in the first sentence that the pronoun takes the place of.

1. Mr. Walters drew a line on the board. He used a blue marker.

2. Christopher and Molly took the bus. They went to the geology museum.

3. The statue is made of stone. It is huge.

4. Jack went to the mall. Sarah met him there.

5. Lulu stepped in the puddle. It was deep.

6. The girls hiked up the trail. A small dog followed them.

7. The boy's shoes were muddy. He cleaned them off.

8. Leah is here. Go and play with her.

9. The antelope lapped at the water. A lion watched it silently.

10. What is wrong with these chips? They taste funny.

Name: _____   **Date:** _____

A pronoun takes the place of a noun or nouns in a sentence.

The subject pronouns *I, we, you, he, she, it,* and *they* can be used as the subject of a sentence.

Nouns
Andre turned the key.
The door opened.
His friends were there.

Pronouns
He turned the key.
It opened.
They were there.

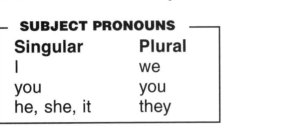

SUBJECT PRONOUNS	
Singular	**Plural**
I	we
you	you
he, she, it	they

Directions: What subject pronoun can take the place of the underlined word or words? Write it on the line.

1. <u>Matt and I</u> found our seats on the plane. _____

2. <u>Our seats</u> were by the window. _____

3. Matt said, "<u>You and I</u> will be able to see everything!" _____

4. There was a woman in the seat beside us. <u>The woman</u> helped us fasten our seatbelts. _____

5. <u>All the flight attendants</u> were friendly. _____

Directions: Using a colored pencil or pen, underline the subject pronouns in this passage.

My friends and I climbed aboard the airplane. This was our first trip on an airplane, and we were very excited. The plane rolled down the runway. Then it rose into the air! It was very  noisy. Later, the flight attendant came by. He offered drinks and snacks. I was too excited to eat anything, but my friends were not. They got juice and pretzels.

Name: _____ **Date:** _____

The pronouns *me, you, him, her, it, us,* and *them* are called object pronouns.
Object pronouns come after action verbs and words such as *to, for, at,* and *with.*

SUBJECT PRONOUNS	
I	it
you	we
he	you
she	they

OBJECT PRONOUNS	
me	it
you	us
him	you
her	them

Directions: What object pronoun can replace the underlined word or words in each sentence? Write the pronoun on the line.

1. Jordy invited <u>the teachers</u> to the concert. _____

2. The tourists took pictures of <u>the monument</u>. _____

3. Marty told a joke to <u>Cooper and me</u>. _____

4. I told the joke to <u>my dad</u>. _____

5. The little pig waddled up to <u>Vickie and Jim</u>. _____

6. Vickie gave <u>the pig</u> an apple. _____

7. Mrs. Chen made lunch for <u>Alysha and me</u>. _____

8. I remembered to thank <u>Mrs. Chen</u> when I left. _____

9. Put the plant in the sun and water <u>the plant</u> every day. _____

10. All the players wear <u>these uniforms</u>. _____

Name: _____   Date: _____

Sometimes you may have trouble deciding whether to use *I* or *me* in a sentence. For example, it can be hard to decide whether to say *Max and me go* or *Max and I go.*

This simple test can help you decide which pronoun to use. Remove *Max* from the first sentence. It is not correct to say, "Me go." It is correct to say, "I go." So it is also correct to say "Max and I go."

Remember that *I* can be used as a subject of a sentence. *Me* is an object pronoun and should be used after action verbs and words such as *at, for, with,* and *to.*

Subject Pronoun: Max and I go to practice.

Object Pronoun: The coach teaches Max and me.

Directions: Complete each sentence by writing *I* or *me* on the line.

1. Jen and _____ found a quarter.

2. This ball belongs to my sister and _____.

3. Ralph told Lisa and _____ about the play.

4. Scruffy brought the tennis ball to Ben and _____.

5. Claire and _____ both have red hair.

6. Liana, Claire, and _____ are cousins.

7. Mom and Dad built a playhouse for Josh, Clay, and _____.

8. You and _____ should join the music group.

9. Amy brought a book for Jeff and _____.

10. He and _____ both love to read.

You have learned that possessive nouns, such as *Ashley's,* show ownership. A **possessive pronoun** can be also used to show ownership.

Nouns
Ashley's brother called.
This is **Ramone's** room.
The **horses'** barn is clean.

Pronouns
Her brother called.
This is **his** room.
Their barn is clean.

POSSESSIVE PRONOUNS

Singular	Plural
my	our
your	your
her, his, its	their

Directions: Underline the possessive pronoun in each sentence.

1. Our clubhouse needs to be cleaned.

2. Phillip will wash its windows.

3. I will sweep the floor with my broom.

4. Can you bring your vacuum cleaner?

5. Sandra will use her tools to fix the door.

Directions: Decide what possessive pronoun can replace the underlined word or words in each sentence. Write the new sentence on the line.

6. This is <u>Ethan's</u> new book about animals.

_____

7. Ethan flips through <u>the book's</u> pages slowly.

_____

8. Anteaters use <u>anteaters'</u> sticky tongues to pick up ants.

_____

9. A skunk lifts <u>a skunk's</u> tail to warn others to stay away.

_____

10. A mother kangaroo carries <u>a mother kangaroo's</u> baby in a pouch.

_____

Name: _____   **Date:** _____

Directions: Read the paragraph. Some pronouns are missing. Write a pronoun from the box on each line. Use each pronoun one time.

it	my	I	them	we

My friends and _____ hiked north of the steep hills, where few have traveled. We were tired and our feet were aching. We were all hungry. I took a loaf of bread from _____ backpack. I shared _____ with the group. While we sat and munched, _____ stared at the mountains in the distance. We would climb _____ tomorrow.

Directions: Decide what pronoun can replace the underlined word or words in each sentence. Write the pronoun on the line.

1. The mountains looked huge. _____
2. I was glad we brought food with my friends and me. _____
3. My friends rested my friends' feet. _____
4. Rita got out Rita's tent. _____
5. I helped Rita put it up. _____

Name: _____ **Date:** _____

You have learned that every sentence has a subject and a predicate. The predicate tells what the subject is or does. The main word in the predicate is a verb. Verbs show action. **Action verbs** show what a person or thing does.

The tree **grows** tall. Acorns **fall** off the branches.
The tree **provides** food and shelter for animals.

Directions: Underline the action verb in each sentence.

1. Hank and Bowser stomp on the flowers in the Davidson's garden.
2. They sleep in the petunia bed.
3. Hank chases the birds from the birdbath.
4. Bowser chews up the garden hose.
5. Mrs. Davidson yells at them every day!

Directions: Underline the complete predicate in each sentence. Circle the action verbs.

6. Mr. Davidson goes to the lumber yard.
7. He buys a big stack of boards.
8. Mr. Davidson measures each board.
9. Mrs. Davidson cuts the boards with an electric saw.
10. Together they build a fence for the dogs.

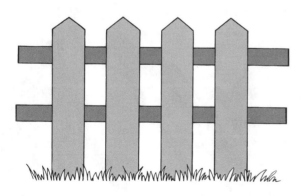

Name: _____   **Date:** _____

Sometimes a verb can be made up of two words: a **helping verb** followed by a **main verb**. The main verb is the most important verb.

Herman **is** <u>practicing</u> for a concert.
He **has** <u>learned</u> his song.
He **will** <u>play</u> his trumpet.

In these sentences, the main verbs are *practicing, learned,* and *play.* The helping verbs are *is, has,* and *will.* Some other common helping verbs are *am, are, was, were, have,* and *had.*

Directions: Underline the helping verb in each sentence. Draw a circle around the main verb.

1. Brianna has finished her homework.

2. We are going to the park.

3. The players were wearing new uniforms.

4. Nelson had read the article before.

5. My new T shirt has faded already.

6. One wheel has fallen off the cart.

7. Your new jeans will become softer with time.

8. The Summer Olympics are held every four years.

9. A red light is flashing on the dashboard.

10. I am playing in the chess tournament next week.

Present tense verbs show action that is happening now.

Troy **puts** a bandage on his knee.

Add –s to the verb if the subject is a singular noun or *he, she,* or *it.*

Tracy **jumps**. She **laughs**.

Do not add –s if the subject is a plural noun or *I, we, you,* or *they.*

Girls **clap**. They **cheer**.

Directions: Circle the correct form of the verb in parentheses.

1. A huge tent (stand, stands) in the field.
2. Families (buy, buys) tickets at the window.
3. A woman (take, takes) the tickets at the entrance.
4. Children (stare, stares) in wonder at the sights.
5. White horses (prance, prances) in the center ring.
6. An elephant (wear, wears) a feathered headdress.
7. A woman (ride, rides) on its back.
8. Acrobats (swing, swings) on trapezes.
9. A clown (pedal, pedals) a tiny bicycle.
10. More clowns (ride, rides) in a tiny car.
11. The crowd (laugh and cheer, laughs and cheers).

Name: _____   **Date:** _____

When a verb is in the present tense, you must make sure it agrees with the subject pronoun of the sentence. The subject pronoun and the verb must both be singular or both be plural.

She <u>sings</u> in the band.
They <u>sing</u> in the band.

Directions: Choose the correct form of the verb.
Write the verb in the space.

1. He _____ on his cleats before the game. (put, puts)

2. I _____ costumes for the dance team. (sew, sews)

3. They _____ delicious pizza. (make, makes)

4. She _____ red paint on the old bicycle. (spray, sprays)

5. We _____ glue instead of tape on our projects. (use, uses)

Directions: Write a verb from the box on each line. Use each verb only once.
Make sure the pronoun and verb agree.

talks	greet	solves	rest	observes

6. They _____.

7. He _____.

8. We _____.

9. She _____.

10. It _____.

You add *–s* to most present tense verbs if the subject of the verb is a singular noun or *he, she,* or *it.* However, if a verb ends with *–s, –sh, –ch, –z,* or *–x,* you must add *–es.*

Hernando tosses.　　　Keisha catches.

If a verb ends with a consonant + *y,* change the *y* to *i* and add *–es.*

study—studies　　　worry—worries　　　fly—flies

Directions: Write the correct form of the verb in parentheses on the line.

1. Jan _____ the ball. (watch)

2. The baker _____ the dough. (mix)

3. Amy _____ for a peach. (reach)

4. This cloth _____ quickly. (dry)

5. Mom _____ her keys in a little green purse. (carry)

6. April _____ her grandparents. (miss)

7. Mason _____ to be on time. (rush)

8. An airplane _____ overhead. (fly)

9. Ray _____ the elevator button. (push)

10. A bee _____ in the honeysuckle. (buzz)

Singular subjects need singular verbs. Plural subjects need plural verbs.

She takes.   We take.   It rolls.   They roll.

Directions: Write the correct form of the verb in parentheses on the line.
The verbs may end in –s, –es, –ies, or have no ending.

1. Shelby's mom _____ us to the game. (drive)

2. The red car _____ the blue truck on the
   highway. (pass)

3. All the players _____ every weekend.
   (practice)

4. The repair company _____ washers and dryers. (fix)

5. Terry and I _____ we could stay up late tonight. (wish)

6. Most students _____ uniforms with yellow shirts. (wear)

7. Jordan _____ to be the class president this year. (want)

8. Mrs. Maxwell and Mr. Campos _____ the students prepare for
   the spelling bee. (help)

9. The big red ants _____ to pick up the cake crumbs. (scurry)

10. My brother _____ Spanish at Lincoln Elementary School. (teach)

Future tense verbs show action that is going to happen in the future. Form the future tense by using the helping verb *will* followed by a verb.

Sherry <u>will</u> want a cold drink when she finishes mowing the lawn.

Directions: Complete the sentences by writing the future tense form of the verb in parentheses.

1. Bailey _____ as soon as he lands his space ship. (call)

2. Kenny _____ up the cookie crumbs. (clean)

3. No one _____ you in that wig. (recognize)

4. Lola _____ the books to the library. (return)

5. They _____ the winner of the barbecue contest tomorrow. (announce)

Directions: Write a sentence in the future tense for each verb.

6. (join) _____

7. (plan) _____

8. (vote) _____

9. (swim) _____

10. (cook) _____

Past tense verbs show actions that have already happened. Most past tense verbs end in –ed. However, some verbs need a spelling change before adding –ed.

If a verb ends in –e, drop the –e and add –ed.

  rake—raked   pose—posed

If a verb ends with a consonant + y, change the y to i and add –ed.

  carry—carried   fry—fried

If a verb ends with one vowel followed by one consonant, double the consonant and add –ed.

  tap—tapped   trot—trotted

Directions: Write the past tense form of each verb.

1. stop _____

2. hop _____

3. obey _____

4. glue _____

5. color _____

6. tidy _____

7. tickle _____

8. marry _____

9. spray _____

10. hope _____

Directions: Rewrite these sentences in the past tense.

11. The ink smears on the paper.

_____

12. The river supplies the town with water.

_____

13. The dogs beg for a piece of bacon.

_____

14. Those wolves howl at the moon all night.

_____

15. Uncle Peter bakes the pumpkin pie.

_____

Name: _____   **Date:** _____

Directions: Write the correct form of the verb in parentheses on the line.

1. Harriet (stroll) _____ down the shady avenue.

2. Suddenly, she (slip) _____ on a banana peel!

3. Her drink (spill) _____ on her jacket.

4. Harriet (stomp) _____ her foot in frustration.

5. She (grab) _____ a tissue from her pocket.

6. She (wipe) _____ up the spill with a tissue.

7. She (spy) _____ a trash can at the bus stop.

8. She (hurry) _____ to throw the wet tissue away.

9. But then she (trip) _____ on a rock and (scrape) _____ her knee.

10. She (sigh) _____ and (limp) _____ home.

BONUS: Write 2–3 sentences about what you did last weekend. Be sure to use the past tense of verbs.

_____

_____

_____

_____

_____

68 Language Arts Skills & Strategies, Level 4 • Saddleback Publishing, Inc. ©2005 • 3 Watson, Irvine, CA 92618 • Phone (888) 735-2225 • www.sdlback.com

Helping verbs can also show action that has already happened. Use the helping verb *has, have,* or *had* with the past tense form of most verbs.

Use *has* with singular subjects. Use *have* with plural subjects.

We have hiked on these trails. He has followed us.

Use *had* with singular and plural subjects.

The rain had stopped. The clouds had disappeared.

Directions: Underline the helping verb in each sentence. Circle the main verb.

1. She had ripped a hole in her sleeve.

2. They have stayed too long.

3. The movie has started already.

4. The boys had already packed their bags.

5. It has rained every day for a week.

Directions: Complete each sentence by writing *has* or *have* and the past tense form of the word in parentheses on the line.

6. The garden _____ a lot in one week. (change)

7. The rosebush _____ its tiny buds. (open)

8. The tomatoes _____ green leaves. (sprout)

9. Birds _____ away all the berries. (carry)

10. Rabbits _____ all the lettuce. (trim)

An **irregular verb** is a verb that does not take *–ed* in the past tense.
Irregular verbs have special past tense spellings that must be remembered.

PRESENT	PAST	WITH *HAS, HAVE* OR *HAD*
fly, flies	flew	(has, have, had) flown
know, knows	knew	(has, have, had) known
throw, throws	threw	(has, have, had) thrown
grow, grows	grew	(has, have, had) grown

Directions: Complete each sentence by writing the correct past tense form of the verb in parentheses on the line.

1. The baby birds have _____ from their nest.
   (fly)

2. Tanya _____ the answer to the question.
   (know)

3. Pam has _____ the broken plate away.
   (throw)

4. Mr. Jordan _____ a giant pumpkin last year.
   (grow)

5. The sailor _____ the rope to the captain. (throw)

6. The pilot had _____ this type of plane before. (fly)

7. Jason and Grant have _____ each other a long time. (know)

8. This plant _____ faster than the other. (grow)

9. Grandpa _____ the paper airplanes across the room. (fly)

10. Tim has _____ three inches this year. (grow)

Name: _____   Date: _____

The verbs *begin, break,* and *wear* have special spellings in the past tense. They have different spellings with *has, have,* or *had.*

PRESENT	PAST	WITH *HAS, HAVE* OR *HAD*
begin, begins	began	(has, have, had) begun
break, breaks	broke	(has, have, had) broken
wear, wears	wore	(has, have, had) worn

Directions: Complete each sentence by writing the correct past tense form of the verb in parentheses on the line.

1. Lola has _____ training for the Olympics. (begin)

2. She has already _____ many track records. (break)

3. Lola _____ running when she was a little girl. (begin)

4. She has _____ out many pairs of running shoes since then! (wear)

5. Lola says, "I won't rest until I have _____ a gold medal!" (wear)

6. Lola _____ her favorite necklace during her first race. (wear)

7. Her mother had _____ it to her from Mexico. (bring)

8. Lola has _____ it in every race since then. (wear)

9. One day the necklace _____, so Lola carried it during the race. (break)

10. She says she _____ the necklace to bring her good luck. (wear)

Name: _____   Date: _____

The verbs *find, say, make,* and *tell* have special spellings in the past tense. They have the same spellings with *has, have,* or *had.*

PRESENT	PAST	WITH *HAS, HAVE* OR *HAD*
find, finds	found	(has, have, had) found
say, says	said	(has, have, had) said
make, makes	made	(has, have, had) made
tell, tells	told	(has, have, had) told

Directions: Complete each sentence by writing the correct past tense form of the verb in parentheses on the line.

1. Troy and Cameron _____ an old chest in Grandma's attic. (find)

2. Grandma had _____ them they could play with anything there. (tell)

3. So Troy opened the lock with a key he had _____ earlier. (find)

4. "It's full of wooden toys!" he _____. (say)

5. Cameron _____, "They look hand carved." (say)

6. Troy wondered who had _____ the toys. (make)

7. Troy and Cameron _____ Grandma about the chest of toys. (tell)

8. Cameron asked, "Who _____ these toys?" (make)

9. Grandma smiled and _____ them about Uncle Victor's talent. (tell)

10. He had _____ the toys in 1955 for his little brothers. (make)

Name: _____   **Date:** _____

The verb *be* does not show action. It tells what someone or something is or is like. This verb has special spellings. Study the chart.

SUBJECT	PRESENT	PAST
I	am	was
he, she, it	is	was
singular nouns	is	was
you, we, they	are	were
plural nouns	are	were

She is a ranger. The park is big.
The party was over. They were tired.

Directions: Circle the correct verb in parentheses.

1. Today (is, are) Saturday.

2. Jorge and Leo (was, were) at the library all day.

3. The library (is, are) on Oakland Avenue.

4. Many people (was, were) there.

5. Mr. Solomon (am, is) the head librarian.

6. All the librarians (is, are) very helpful.

7. Jorge and Leo (is, are) curious about submarines.

8. It (was, were) easy to find information.

9. Several books (was, were) about ships and submarines.

10. I (am, are) interested in them, too.

Name: _____   **Date:** _____

Adjectives are words that describe nouns or pronouns. They can describe and give more information about a person, place, or thing.

Some adjectives tell *what kind.* Other adjectives tell *how many.* Both kinds usually come before the word they describe.

This is an **easy** recipe. (*Easy* tells what kind of recipe.)
You need **two** eggs to make it. (*Two* tells how many eggs.)

Directions: Write the adjective or adjectives that describe the underlined noun in each sentence.

1. Simon found an interesting <u>insect</u> today. _____

2. It had a shiny green <u>shell</u>. _____

3. Simon put it in a jar with some <u>leaves</u>. _____

4. The insect wiggled its long <u>antennae</u>. _____

5. Simon watched the insect for several <u>minutes</u> and then let it go. _____

Directions: Underline each adjective. Draw an arrow to the noun it describes.

6. Two students gave a report about walking sticks today.

7. They are strange insects!

8. They have long, thin bodies that look like sticks.

9. They can give off a stinky odor when they are attacked.

10. If they lose a leg, they can grow a new leg to replace it.

BONUS: Write a sentence describing an insect you have seen. Circle each adjective and draw an arrow to the noun it describes.

_____

_____

_____

Name: _____   **Date:** _____

Adjectives usually come before the words they describe. However, sometimes adjectives come after the words they describe. When they do, they usually follow a form of the verb *be*.

The rain **is cold**. My jacket **is wet**.

Directions: Write each adjective and the noun or pronoun it describes.

1. The weather was gloomy. _____ _____

2. The sky was gray. _____ _____

3. Kayla's shoes were wet from the rain. _____ _____

4. She was chilly. _____ _____

5. The fireplace was cheerful. _____ _____

6. The armchair was cozy. _____ _____

7. Soon, Kayla's feet were warm. _____ _____

8. She was sleepy. _____ _____

9. Her eyelids were heavy. _____ _____

10. Her dreams were sweet! _____ _____

A, an, and *the* are special adjectives called **articles**. Singular nouns use *a* and *an.* If the word after the article begins with a consonant sound, use *a.* If the word after the article begins with a vowel sound, use *an.*

> **An eagle** and **a hawk** soared above us.
> **An anxious** rabbit ran away.

You can use *the* with any noun. The noun can be singular or plural.

> **The hungry seagull** stole my sandwich.
> **The ants** took the rest.

Directions: Circle the correct article in parentheses.

1. (a, an) apple
2. (a, an) orange cat
3. (an, the) sleepy dog
4. (a, an) hobby
5. (an, the) green shirt

6. (an, the) old newspapers
7. (a, an) tall glass
8. (a, an) wheel
9. (an, the) white envelopes
10. (a, an) ordinary day

Directions: Choose the correct article in parentheses. Write it on the line.

11. _____ penny saved is a penny earned. (A, An)
12. _____ book is like a garden carried in the pocket. (A, An)
13. The grass is always greener on _____ other side. (a, the)
14. An apple a day keeps _____ doctor away. (the, an)
15. Life is like _____ bowl of cherries. (a, an)

Adjectives can tell how people, places, or things are alike or different. They can be used to compare nouns.

Add –er to most adjectives to compare two nouns. Add –est to most adjectives when you compare three or more nouns.

> Greg has a **big** sandwich.
> Amy's sandwich is **bigger** than his.
> My sandwich is the **biggest** of all three.

Some adjectives need a spelling change before adding –er or –est.

If the adjective ends in –e, drop the –e and add the ending.

> nice—nicer—nicest

If the adjective ends with a consonant + y, change the y to i and add the ending.

> tiny—tinier—tiniest

If the adjective ends with one vowel followed by one consonant, double the consonant and add the ending.

> red—redder—reddest

Directions: Underline the correct form of the adjective in parentheses.

1. Raul thinks art is the (nicer, nicest) class at school.

2. Amy's painting is (smaller, smallest) than Brittany's.

3. These paints are (brighter, brightest) than the old ones.

4. The paste is (thicker, thickest) than the glue.

5. It is the (easier, easiest) to use.

6. Is your brush (wider, widest) than mine?

7. Yes, this is the (wider, widest) of all ten brushes.

8. Your clay pot is (drier, driest) than it was yesterday.

9. The clay has gotten (harder, hardest).

10. Nick has drawn the (funnier, funniest) cartoon ever!

Name: _____ **Date:** _____

Directions: Complete each sentence by writing the correct form of the adjective in parentheses on the line.

1. That rabbit has the _____ ears I have ever seen! (floppy)

2. July is usually _____ than June. (hot)

3. Are owls really _____ than other birds? (wise)

4. This bread is _____ than the biscuits. (chewy)

5. The _____ toy for a baby is one without small parts. (safe)

6. We chose the _____ of all the wallpaper for our dollhouse. (pretty)

7. This pen makes a _____ line than the marker does. (thin)

8. My dog is _____ than my cat. (friendly)

9. The blue sweater is _____ than the red sweater. (soft)

10. I think this is the _____ song in the world. (sad)

Name: _____   **Date:** _____

You cannot add *–er* and *–est* to all adjectives. If an adjective is long, use the word *more* or *most* to compare things.

> Greg has a **delicious** sandwich.
> Amy's sandwich is **more delicious** than his.
> My sandwich is the **most delicious** of all three.

Do not add *–er* or *–est* and *more* or *most* to the same adjective.

> **Incorrect:** This crossword puzzle is *more harder* than the maze.
> This crossword puzzle is the *most difficultest* of all.
>
> **Correct:** This crossword puzzle is **harder** than the maze.
> This crossword puzzle is the **most difficult** of all.

Directions: Complete each sentence by writing *more* or *most* on the line.

1. Grandpa told us the _____ amazing story today.

2. It was about the _____ dangerous trip he ever went on.

3. This trip was _____ exciting than his trip to the rain forest.

4. On this trip, he climbed the _____ rugged mountains in the world.

5. He said it was even _____ challenging than his swim across the ocean.

Directions: Complete each sentence by writing *more* or *most* plus the adjective in parentheses.

6. I think the octopus is the _____ animal in the world. (interesting)

7. Its eight arms make it look _____ than other sea creatures. (unusual)

8. It is the _____ swimmer in the ocean. (graceful)

9. Because it has no bones, it is _____ than other creatures. (flexible)

10. It is also _____ than many animals. (intelligent)

Name: _____ **Date:** _____

The adjectives *good* and *bad* have special forms for comparing.

good, better, best

Rodney saw a **good** movie last night.
It was **better** than the movie he saw last week.
He says it was the **best** movie he has ever seen.

bad, worse, worst

I heard a **bad** song by R. U. Howling.
It was **worse** than the last song he wrote.
What is the **worst** song you have ever heard?

Directions: Write the correct comparative form of the adjective in parentheses.

1. This is the _____ cold I have ever had. (bad)

2. I feel _____ now than when I had the mumps last year. (bad)

3. I hope I will feel _____ tomorrow. (good)

4. I feel _____ when I think about my friends. (bad)

5. My friends are having a _____ time than I am right now. (good)

6. Because I am sick, I missed the _____ game of the season. (good)

7. The _____ part about having a cold is the coughing. (bad)

8. Sneezing feels _____ than coughing. (good)

9. Mom and Dad say the _____ cure for a cold is rest. (good)

10. Resting is _____ when I do not cough. (good)

Name: _____   **Date:** _____

Directions: Underline the adjectives in each sentence. Draw an arrow to the nouns they describe.

1. I am sorry that I stepped on your sore toe.

2. The ice cream is runny after sitting in the hot sun.

3. Renee was nervous because she had to give an important speech.

4. Derek was grateful for the wonderful present.

5. The car was stuck in the deep mud.

Directions: Complete each sentence by writing the correct form of the adjective in parentheses on the line.

6. Of all the players, Gretchen is the _____. (confident).

7. Is the hummingbird the _____ of all birds? (tiny)

8. Walking sticks look _____ than beetles. (strange)

9. This fresh bread is _____ than those old bagels. (good)

10. This is the _____ weather we have had all week. (bad)

Name: _____   **Date:** _____

You have learned that adjectives are words that describe nouns and pronouns. An **adverb** is a word that describes a verb. It can tell *how, when,* or *where.* An adverb can come before or after the word it describes.

How: Tom **quickly** opened the door.
When: **Then** he grabbed a snack.
Where: Tom ran **upstairs**.

There are many adverbs. These are just a few:

How: fast, quietly, gently, happily, softly, smoothly, bravely, sweetly

When: always, never, often, today, tomorrow, yesterday, first, next, then, later, soon, finally

Where: here, there, everywhere, ahead, behind, nearby, away, far, out, in, outside, inside, upstairs

Directions: Write the adverb that describes each underlined verb. Tell whether it tells *how, when,* or *where.*

1. The show finally <u>started</u>. _____

2. Two cars <u>waited</u> nearby. _____

3. Grandma always <u>remembers</u> my birthday. _____

4. Dana <u>read</u> the directions carefully. _____

5. Sometimes I <u>sing</u> to myself. _____

Directions: Write each adverb and the verb it describes.

6. Uncle Theo once lived on a farm. _____

7. Aunt Suzanna worked there with him. _____

8. They always had many chores to do. _____

9. Aunt Suzanna usually milked the cows. _____

10. Uncle Theo carried the heavy buckets easily. _____

Adjectives can be used to compare people, places, or things. Adverbs can be used to compare actions. Add *–er* to short adverbs to compare two actions. Add *–est* to compare three or more actions.

> soon, sooner, soonest
>
> Bill arrived **soon**.
> Victor arrived **sooner** than Bill did.
> Kim arrived the **soonest** of all three.

If an adverb ends with *–ly,* use *more* or *most* to compare.

> The flashlight shines **brightly**.
> It shines **more brightly** than the candle.
> The lamp shines the **most brightly** of all three.

If you use *–er* or *–est*, do not use *more* or *most.*

Directions: Complete each sentence by writing *more* or *most* plus the adverb in parentheses.

1. Kiera sings _____ than Toby. (sweetly)

2. Brandon can sing _____ than Kevin. (low)

3. Gordon strums his guitar _____ than Bryan. (gently)

4. Kanesha can sing _____ of all ten girls. (high)

5. Stacy thumps her kettle drum _____ than the other drummers. (hard)

6. Mario's trumpet blares _____ of all the horns. (loudly)

7. Stan is clapping _____ than all the others. (fast)

8. The director will ask him to clap _____. (slowly)

9. Tonight's practice will last _____ than last night's. (long)

10. The director hopes the students will play _____ than before. (carefully)

Name: _____   **Date:** _____

It is easy to confuse *good* and *well*. *Good* is an adjective that describes nouns. *Well* is an adverb that describes verbs.

Adjective

Amy is a good musician.

Adverb

She plays the piano well.

Good is also used with certain sense verbs, such as *feel, smell, taste,* and *look.*

I feel good today.
That pizza smells good.
It tastes good, too.

Directions: Underline the word that correctly completes each sentence.

1. Taylor is (good, well) at singing.

2. He sang (good, well) at the audition.

3. I hope I can skate as (good, well) as you someday.

4. Our picnic was not (good, well).

5. It started (good, well), but then it rained.

6. The radio you made with Uncle Chester works really (good, well).

7. Dion cooks really (good, well).

8. These oatmeal raisin cookies are (good, well).

9. This story is about a (good, well) king.

10. He treats his people (good, well).

BONUS: Write a sentence that uses both *good* and *well* correctly.

_____

_____

_____

Name: _____ **Date:** _____

Directions: Complete each sentence by writing *more* or *most* plus the adverb in parentheses.

1. Xavier colored his picture _____ than James did. (neatly)

2. The watercolor paint dries _____ than the oil paint. (fast)

3. James uses color the _____ of all the art students. (creatively)

4. Selena molds the clay _____ than I do. (skillfully)

5. I think sculpting is the _____ of all the activities. (hard)

Directions: Complete each sentence by writing *good* or *well*.

6. Megan is a _____ artist.

7. She can paint and draw very _____.

8. I think this painting is really _____.

9. She did a _____ job of showing the details.

10. I like it _____ enough to buy it!

BONUS: Write two sentences comparing two pieces of art or two artists. Use adverbs to compare.

_____

_____

_____

_____

_____

_____

Name: _____   **Date:** _____

The words *not, no, no one, nobody, nothing, none, nowhere,* and *never* are **negatives**. Contractions made with *not* are also negatives. These words give sentences a negative meaning.

> **Nobody** called. I **didn't** talk to anybody.

Never use two negatives together.

> **Incorrect:** We don't have no tickets.
> We can't never go on a ride.
> **Correct:** We don't have any tickets.
> We can't ever go on a ride.

Directions: Write the word that correctly completes the sentence.

1. Hillary didn't eat _____ cotton candy. (any, no)

2. Bill hasn't _____ ridden on the Ferris wheel. (never, ever)

3. Chelsea didn't win _____ gold fish in the ring toss. (any, none)

4. I haven't _____ gotten scared in the Fun House. (ever, never)

5. She couldn't find _____ to go with her on the rollercoaster. (anybody, nobody)

6. Rachel couldn't find her hat _____ after she got off the Scrambler. (nowhere, anywhere)

7. The grumpy clown didn't blow up _____ balloons. (any, no)

8. Nothing _____ (never, ever) makes him smile.

9. He never gives _____ a free balloon. (no one, anyone)

10. This fair wasn't _____ fun at all! (no, any)

Name: _____ **Date:** _____

A prefix is a group of letters that can be put at the beginning of a word. A prefix changes the meaning of a word.

I think this is a nice painting. Luke **disagrees**. He **dislikes** it.

PREFIX	MEANING	EXAMPLE	MEANING
re–	again	reread	read again
dis–	not; opposite of	dislike	not like
over–	too much	overheat	heat too much

Directions: Complete the chart by adding *re–*, *dis–*, or *over–* to the word in the first column. The new word should have the meaning listed in the second column.

PREFIX + WORD	MEANING
1. _____open	open again
2. _____work	work too much
3. _____respect	not respect
4. _____do	do too much
5. _____approve	not approve

Directions: Complete each sentence by adding *re–*, *dis–*, or *over–* to the word in parentheses.

6. I need to correct some mistakes on my paper, so I will _____ it. (write)

7. If you run around in the hot sun, you may get _____. (heated)

8. Mom told Roman not to touch the cake, but Roman _____ and stuck his finger in the icing. (obeyed)

9. If you _____ the basket with apples, it will be too heavy to carry. (load)

10. Telling a lie is a _____ thing to do. (honest)

Name: _____   **Date:** _____

Like a prefix, a suffix changes the meaning of a word. However, a suffix is added at the end of the word.

> Dogs are **adaptable** creatures. They can adapt to life in many different environments.

SUFFIX	MEANING	EXAMPLE	MEANING
–ful	full of	fearful	full of fear
–able	can be or can do	acceptable	can be accepted
–less	without	painless	without pain

Directions: Complete the chart by adding –*ful* –*able*, or –*less* to the word in the first column. The new word should have the meaning listed in the second column.

WORD + SUFFIX	MEANING
1. view_____	can be viewed
2. pain_____	full of pain
3. avoid_____	can be avoided
4. understand_____	can be understood
5. hair_____	without hair

Directions: Complete each sentence by adding –*ful*, –*able*, or –*less* to the word in parentheses.

6. The kitten hid under the couch because it was _____ of the growling dog. (fear)

7. This broken vase is _____. I will glue the pieces together. (repair)

8. That broken spoon is _____. Throw it away. (use)

9. My _____ neighbor mowed my lawn when I was sick. (help)

10. The guitar was not _____ because it had no strings. (play)

Name: _____   Date: _____

Homophones are words that are spelled differently but sound alike. The contractions of some pronouns are easily confused with other words because they sound alike. Read the homophones and example sentences below.

Their: *shows ownership*   Is this their house?
There: *at or in that place*   Let's go there.
They're: *they + are*   I hope they're at home.

It's: *it + is OR it + has*   It's a nice watch.
Its: *shows ownership*   Its hands are gold.

You're: *you + are*   You're a good singer.
Your: *shows ownership*   Your voice is beautiful.

Directions: Circle the word in parentheses that completes each sentence correctly.

1. (It's, Its) fun to look at old photographs.

2. (Their, They're) all here in this box.

3. Is this (your, you're) grandparents?

4. (Their, There) names are written on the back.

5. This picture shows how pretty (their, there) house was.

6. The family gathered on (it's, its) porch every evening.

7. They lived (their, there) for 40 years.

8. (Your, You're) just a little baby in this photo.

9. (Its, It's) a cute picture.

10. Look how curly (your, you're) hair was!

Name: _____   **Date:** _____

Homophones are words that are pronounced alike but have a different spelling and meaning. There are many homophones in the English language. Here are just a few:

four, for   our, hour   male, mail   no, know

I brought **four** red flowers **for** you.

Male deer have antlers.   I got a letter in the **mail** today.

Directions: Think of a homophone for each word. Then write one sentence for each word. Use a dictionary if you need help.

1. blew: _____

   _____ : _____

2. ate: _____

   _____ : _____

3. see: _____

   _____ : _____

4. week: _____

   _____ : _____

5. won: _____

   _____ : _____

The following words are sometimes used incorrectly. They may have similar spellings or similar meanings that make them easy to confuse.

WORD	MEANING	EXAMPLE
already all ready	before a particular time all or completely prepared	I have already done the dishes. We are all ready to go on the field trip.
set sit	to put to rest or stay in one place	Set the lamp on my desk, please. Shall we sit on the couch?
lay lie	to put on a flat surface to be in a flat position on a surface	Lay the baby in the crib. Sam lies on the grass.
let leave	to allow to go away from OR to let stay	Mom lets us make popcorn. I will leave at 4:00. Leave the plates on the table.
good well	an adjective that describes nouns an adverb that describes verbs	This is a good song. She sings it well.

Directions: Choose the correct word for each sentence.

1. My little brother has _____ learned to tie his shoe. (already, all ready)

   The sandwiches are _____ to eat. (already, all ready)

2. On rainy days I like to _____ on my bed and read a good book. (lie, lay)

   You should _____ your school clothes out the night before. (lie, lay)

3. He did a _____ job of fixing the bike. (good, well)

   I know Amy very _____. (good, well)

4. Please _____ your papers on my desk. (let, leave)

   Will you _____ me brush your hair? (let, leave)

5. _____ your packages down on the counter. (sit, set)

   Three people can _____ on this big swing. (sit, set)

Name: _____   Date: _____

A **compound word** is made when two words are joined together to form a new word.

Flower + pot = flowerpot

Directions: See how many compound words you can create from these base words.

1. News _____

2. Sun _____

3. Star _____

4. Eye _____

5. Hand _____

6. Some _____

7. Every _____

8. Play _____

9. Thumb _____

10. Lip _____

BONUS: Write two sentences that contain compound words. Try to use as many compound words as you can.

_____

_____

_____

_____

_____

_____

_____

_____

Name: _____ **Date:** _____

Synonyms are words that have the same or nearly the same meaning. You can make your writing more interesting by using synonyms, instead of the same words over and over.

Robbie struggled with the **huge** box.
His arms ached under the **enormous** load.

Huge and *enormous* have nearly the same meaning.

Directions: Read each sentence. Circle the letter of the word that has almost the same meaning as the underlined word in the sentence.

1. Dave told a <u>weird</u> story to the campers. It gave them the creeps.
   a. long
   b. odd
   c. funny

2. <u>Jump</u> over that puddle.
   a. leap
   b. swim
   c. splash

3. The president <u>ordered</u> everyone to stop talking at the club meeting.
   a. asked
   b. commanded
   c. begged

4. This banner is <u>tattered</u>. I can see through the holes!
   a. large
   b. new
   c. torn

5. Shelly <u>laughed</u> at his joke.
   a. smiled
   b. blushed
   c. chuckled

6. I <u>adore</u> my new puppy.
   a. amuse
   b. love
   c. play with

7. It is too <u>cramped</u> in here. Let's find a bigger room.
   a. bright
   b. crowded
   c. dirty

8. Jeff told another <u>lie</u>!
   a. song
   b. fib
   c. truth

9. No one recognized Josh in his <u>disguise</u>.
   a. costume
   b. uniform
   c. suit

10. That crumbling cliff is <u>perilous</u>.
   a. safe
   b. high
   c. dangerous

Antonyms are words that have opposite meanings. *Old* and *young* are antonyms.

right—left	calm—upset	interesting—dull
stop—start	enemy—friend	smile—frown
lost—found	wet—dry	awake—asleep

Directions: Write an antonym for each word. There may be more than one possible antonym for each word.

1. over—_____

2. hard—_____

3. bumpy—_____

4. crooked—_____

5. careful—_____

Directions: Choose the word in parentheses that is an antonym of the underlined word. Rewrite the sentence, using the antonym in place of the underlined word.

6. Henry marched <u>sadly</u> to the office. (cheerfully, angrily)

_____

7. My little sister is usually very <u>quiet</u>. (shy, noisy)

_____

8. Her room is always very <u>tidy</u>. (messy, warm)

_____

9. Allen <u>dislikes</u> playing outside with his friends. (studies, enjoys)

_____

10. Hansel and Gretel were very <u>wise</u> children. (tasty, foolish)

_____

Name: _____   Date: _____

Writers sometimes use figurative language to help create an image in the reader's mind. **Figurative language** is words or phrases that do not mean exactly what they say.

Today **the sun is a bright yellow tennis ball**, bouncing through the sky.

This is an example of figurative language: the sun is not really a tennis ball, but it is *like* a tennis ball because it is round and yellow. This sentence creates an image of the sun in the reader's mind.

Writers can also use **literal language** to describe things. When they use literal language, they use the real meanings of words.

Today **the sun is round and bright yellow**.

Directions: Write *figurative* or *literal* to tell what kind of language the writer has used in the sentences below.

1. Mosquitoes zoomed in on us like tiny black helicopters. _____

2. We could hear an owl hooting in a tree nearby. _____

3. Water dripped slowly from the broken fountain. _____

4. The winter wind sighed through the crack in the window. _____

5. The grass of the coming spring slept peacefully under its blanket of snow. _____

Directions: For each word, write a descriptive sentence using figurative language.

6. stars _____

7. river _____

8. fire _____

9. hair _____

10. silence _____

`Name:` _____   `Date:` _____

Two common kinds of figurative language are similes and metaphors.
A **simile** compares two things using the word *like* or *as.*

> Her face was pale **as the moon**.
> Her face was **like a pale moon**.

A **metaphor** also compares two things, but it does not use the word *like* or *as.*

> Her **pale moon face** stared down at me.

Directions: Write *simile* or *metaphor* to tell what kind of language the writer has used in the sentences below.

1. Bad luck followed me around like a little rain cloud. _____

2. Brad's anger was a hot coal burning in his stomach. _____

3. Lauren was so excited that she bounced around like a rubber ball.

   _____

4. Ma's biscuits were soft clouds of delicious lightness. _____

5. My pillow was a brick. _____

Directions: Complete the similes and metaphors below. Use your imagination.

6. Frank was as tall as _____.

7. My love is _____.

8. Her hair was as red as _____.

9. The team's excitement was like _____.

10. Darkness fell like _____.

Name: _____   **Date:** _____

Personification is another kind of figurative language. When a writer uses personification, he or she gives a human quality to an animal or thing.

The sun **smiled** down on us from above.

This is an example of personification because the sun cannot really smile. The writer writes about the sun "smiling" in order to create the image of a bright sun in the reader's mind. The reader can also tell that the writer feels good about the sun, because "smiled" is a happy, positive word.

Directions: Underline the object being personified in each sentence. Then rewrite the sentence, using literal language to express the main idea of the sentence.

1. The winter wind's bony fingers grabbed my hat from my head.

   _____

2. The teapot sang for us to take her off the stove.

   _____

3. The camera observed the entire scene.

   _____

4. We heard the chocolate cake calling out to us!

   _____

5. The tears kissed his cheeks as they fell.

   _____

BONUS: Write a sentence that personifies one of the following objects or animals: horse, mirror, shadow, fox, water.

_____

_____

Dictionaries give definitions of words. The words are listed in alphabetical order.

The words that are defined are called entry words. They are usually in dark type. The entry word is followed by a pronunciation guide and the part of speech (noun, verb, etc.). The definitions come next. If an entry word has more than one definition, each definition will start with a number. If a word can be more than one part of speech, the dictionary will usually give a definition for each part of speech. Study the sample dictionary entry below.

pronunciation guide   **part of speech**   **definitions**

drape (drāp) *verb* **1:** To dress or hang with cloth in loose folds. **2:** To arrange or let fall in loose folds: *He draped his coat over the chair.* Δ *noun* A curtain.

entry word

Directions: Use the sample dictionary page below to answer the questions.

plot (plŏt) *noun* **1.** A small piece of land used for a specific purpose: *Tomatoes grew in the garden plot.* **2.** The series of events in a play or story. **3.** A secret plan to carry out an evil or illegal action. Δ *verb* **1.** To form a secret plan: *The pirates plotted to steal the gold.* **2.** To locate points on a graph.

plow (plou) *noun* A farm tool with a heavy blade used to break up soil and create rows in soil. Δ *verb* **1.** To break up soil with a plow. **2.** To move forward with difficulty; plod: *We plowed through the deep snow.* **3.** To do something with eagerness and vigor: *Tanya plowed through the exciting book in three days.*

pluck (plŭk) *verb* **1.** To detach by holding and pulling with the fingers; pick: *pluck a flower.* **2.** To pull out the hair or feathers of: *pluck a chicken.* **3.** To pull and release the strings of an instrument to make a sound. Δ *noun* Courage and daring when faced with difficulties: *Henry showed a lot of pluck when he saved the kittens from the burning shed.*

1. Which word names something you do in math class? _____

2. Which word names something a person might do to a turkey? _____

3. Which definition of *plow* fits this sentence? *The farmer plowed the field in early spring.* Write the number of the definition: _____

4. Which definition of *plot* fits this sentence? *I like the characters in this story, but the plot doesn't make sense.* Write the number of the definition: _____

5. Which definition of *pluck* fits this sentence? *David plucked an apple from the tree.* Write the number of the definition: _____

Name: _____   **Date:** _____

Like a dictionary, a thesaurus contains entry words in alphabetical order. However, a thesaurus does not give definitions. Instead, it gives a list of synonyms for each entry word. As you have learned, synonyms are words that have the same or nearly the same meaning. A thesaurus can help make your writing more exciting. You can use it to find the words that express your ideas exactly.

Look at the sample thesaurus entry. The word bad has many shades of meaning. You must read the entry carefully before choosing a synonym that suits your idea.

> **bad** *adjective*
> 1. (of inferior quality) defective, inferior, unsatisfactory, lousy: *a bad phone connection*
> 2. evil, wicked
> 3. naughty, disobedient
> 4. unpleasant, disturbing, terrible: *bad news*
> 5. unappetizing
> 6. rotten, spoiled: *This cheese is bad.*
> 7. severe, serious: *a bad cold*
> 8. sorry, regretful, sad
> 9. sick, ill
> 10. harmful, damaging

Directions: Using the sample thesaurus entry above, complete the sentences by writing a synonym for the word *bad* on each line.

1. Cameron has a _____ case of the flu.

2. This bread is _____. It has green mold growing on it.

3. The _____ king plotted to capture his brother's land.

4. My dog was _____ and tore up a book.

5. I feel _____ that I tore your picture.

6. I think a hotdog with marshmallows would be _____.

7. Most experts say that smoking is _____ for you.

8. This lightbulb is brand new, but it is _____. It does not work.

9. We got the _____ news that Mr. Martin was very sick.

10. Cody feels _____. He has a sore throat and a headache.

Name: _____   **Date:** _____

An **encyclopedia** is a reference book that contains articles on many different people, places, things, and events. You can find encyclopedias in your library or online.

Encyclopedia articles are arranged alphabetically in books. To find a particular article, you must decide what the key word is. The key word is usually what the article is mostly about. For example, if you wanted to find out the temperature of the planet Saturn, you would look up *Saturn. Saturn* is the key word. If you wanted to read about Yellowstone National Park, the key word would be *Yellowstone.*

The books in a set of encyclopedias are called volumes. Each volume is labeled with a letter or letters. The subjects of all the articles in that volume begin with that letter or letters.

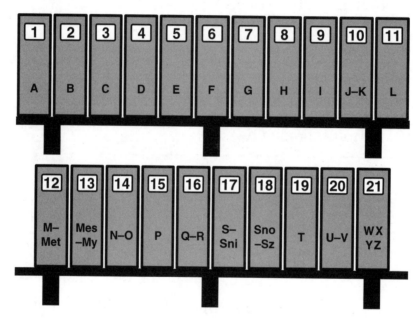

Directions: Which volume of the encyclopedias above would most likely contain the answer to each question? There may be more than one possible answer. Write the volume number or numbers on the line.

1. How does a bat catch insects in the dark? _____

2. Do fish sleep? _____

3. When did Thomas Edison invent the light bulb? _____

4. What does the flag of Japan look like? _____

5. How are steam engines different from gas engines? _____

Name: _____   Date: _____

Some books have special pages that help you find information easily. The **table of contents** is at the front of the book. It lists the names of the chapters and the page number where each chapter begins.

Directions: Here is part of the table of contents of a book called *Guitar Basics.* Use the table of contents to answer the following questions.

1. Which chapter is about styles of music? _____

2. Which chapter would be most important to read before going shopping for a guitar? _____

3. If the author added a section about jazz, which chapter would it belong in? _____

4. On what page does the chapter about taking care of your guitar begin? _____

5. On what page does the section on Blues begin? _____

6. How many pages are in the chapter on choosing a guitar? _____

7. In which chapter would you probably find information on cleaning a guitar? _____

8. Which chapter is most likely to include information about a famous rock guitarist? _____

9. Which chapter is most likely to tell how to play "Mary Had a Little Lamb"? _____

10. Which chapter is most likely to explain what a chord is? _____

Name: _____ **Date:** _____

The **index** is found at the back of the book. It lists the page numbers where you can find information about particular subjects in the book. The subjects are arranged in alphabetical order.

Directions: Here is part of the index of a book called *Guitar Basics.* Write the page number or numbers on which you might find the answers to each question.

INDEX

Cleaning, 5–6
Cloth for wiping your guitar, 5
Fingerpicking, 26
Guitars
   basic description of,
   shopping for, 2
Hand position, 25, 32
Neck of the guitar
   basic description, 15
   repairing, 49–50

Picks
   how to hold, 28
   types of 27
Songs
   "Heart and Soul," 54
   "On Top of Old Smokey," 56
   "You Are My Sunshine," 58
Strings
   buying, 3
   replacing, 6

---

1. How do you play "You Are My Sunshine"? _____

2. What is fingerpicking? _____

3. What should I do if the neck of my guitar breaks? _____

4. How should I hold my hands while playing? _____

5. What kinds of picks are there? _____

6. Which strings should I choose at the store?

   _____

7. What are the basic parts of a guitar? _____

8. What kind of cloth should I use to wipe my guitar?

   _____

9. Should I use water to clean my guitar? _____

10. How do you replace the strings on a guitar?

   _____

Name: _____ **Date:** _____

After you write a paragraph or a paper, it is important to revise your work. When you revise, you read it over and check that each sentence is complete and your ideas are clear. As you know, a complete sentence has a subject and a predicate. A sentence that is missing a subject or a predicate is called a **sentence fragment**. Sometimes you can fix a sentence fragment by adding it to another sentence.

Hummingbirds can fly backwards. And hover in one place.

And hover in one place is not a complete sentence. Fix it by adding it to the first sentence.

Hummingbirds can fly backwards and hover in one place.

Directions: Fix the incomplete sentences by adding them to the complete sentences.

1. Hummingbirds have thin beaks. And long, thin tongues.

   _____

2. They fly to a flower. Then sip the nectar.

   _____

3. They lap it up. With their long tongues.

   _____

4. They have tiny wings. That beat hundreds of times per minute.

   _____

5. They have to eat a lot. Because of the amount of energy they burn.

   _____

6. They sip at the flowers. While hovering in one place.

   _____

7. I saw one yesterday. By the honeysuckle bush.

   _____

8. You can really hear a humming noise. From their beating wings.

   _____

9. Hummingbirds are tiny. But very fierce.

   _____

10. They will defend their area. From other birds.

    _____

Name: _____ **Date:** _____

Directions: This story contains five sentence fragments. Find them and correct them. Write the new sentences on the lines below.

Once upon a time, there were two little goats. They lived near a rickety old bridge. The bridge went across a little river. Beautiful grass grew on the other side of the river. The two goats longed to eat the grass. On the other side of the river. Unfortunately, a grumpy troll lived under the bridge. He was mean. And yelled a lot. Every time

the goats tried to cross the bridge, the troll would stop them. The little goats grew thin. Finally, the hungry goats decided to call Thor. Thor was the biggest goat in the land. He was six feet tall. With long, sharp horns. Thor was happy to help his scrawny friends. He clopped over to the bridge and called to the troll, "Come out now, you hobgoblin!"

"I'm no hobgoblin," yelled Fester. "I'm a troll and you are trespassing on my bridge. Get off before I scare you silly!"

Thor just laughed. And stomped his feet. This shook the bridge and the troll, too. Then Thor scooped up the troll. With his steely horns. He tossed him into the air and kicked him far, far away. The two little goats cheered their hero and they all had a delicious dinner of tasty, fresh grass.

1. _____
2. _____
3. _____
4. _____
5. _____

Name: _____ **Date:** _____

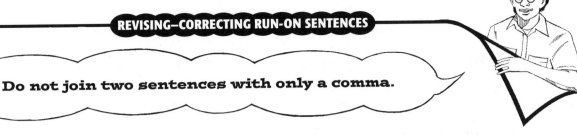

Do not join two sentences with only a comma.

A run-on sentence is made up of two sentences written as though they were one sentence. One way to correct a run-on sentence is to write each complete thought as a separate sentence.

Run-on: I like biking better than walking, I can go much faster.
Correct: I like biking better than walking. I can go much faster.

Another way to fix it is to join the two complete thoughts in a way that is correct.
Correct: I like biking better than walking because I can go much faster.

Directions: Correct each run-on sentence by separating the two complete thoughts into two sentences or by joining them correctly.

1. I love raccoons, they are my favorite animal.

_____

2. Their faces are so cute, they look like they're wearing a mask.

_____

3. Their tails are bushy they have rings.

_____

4. You have probably seen one, they live everywhere.

_____

5. They can live in the forest they can live in towns.

_____

6. Sometimes they cause trouble, they open garbage cans.

_____

7. They will eat almost anything, they will even eat food scraps.

_____

8. They like to eat fish and crawdads, they love berries and sweet corn.

_____

9. They have a funny habit, they often dip their food in water before eating.

_____

10. Be careful if you see a sick raccoon, it may have rabies.

_____

Name: _____ **Date:** _____

Directions: This paragraph contains five run-on sentences. Find them and fix them. Rewrite the paragraph correctly on the lines.

My favorite singer is David Winslow. He has a great voice, his songs are beautiful. My sister is so lucky. She got to meet him last week! She works at a restaurant she is a waitress. Well, one day last week David Winslow came to eat there. My sister waited on him. She said she got very nervous, her hands were shaking. He ordered spaghetti. My sister was so nervous that she forgot to bring him a fork! He was nice he didn't get mad. But then she spilled water on him. She was very embarrassed, he still wasn't angry. He even gave her his autograph.

_____

_____

_____

_____

_____

_____

_____

_____

_____

_____

_____

_____

_____

_____

_____

_____

_____

Name: _____ **Date:** _____

After you write a paragraph or a paper, it is important to read it over to check that each sentence is complete and your ideas are clear. Another thing to look out for is too many short, choppy sentences. They can make your writing seem dull.

Short, choppy sentences can be improved in several ways. One way is to join short sentences to make longer compound sentences. If the ideas in the sentences are related, combine them with a comma and the word *and, but,* or *or.* Creating compound sentences can help make your writing smooth and easy to read.

CHOPPY: Dylan has a boat. He loves to sail.
SMOOTH: Dylan has a boat, and he loves to sail.

Directions: Read the story. Combine each pair of underlined sentences to create compound sentences. Write the new sentences on the lines below.

Waldo had a guppy named Mortimer. One day, Waldo heard Mortimer whimper. Waldo sat by Mortimer's bowl. He looked at the guppy. "What's wrong?" he asked.

The guppy sighed. A tear rolled down his cheek. "All day I swim around and around, all by myself."

Mortimer was lonely. He needed a friend. "I'm sorry!" cried Waldo. "I know just what we should do." Waldo picked up the fish bowl. They went to the pet store.

The shopkeeper smiled. He greeted them. "What are you looking for?" he asked.

Waldo explained how lonely Mortimer was. The shopkeeper had an idea. It was not a good one. "How about a playful puppy for your guppy?" he suggested.

Waldo frowned. He shook his head.

"Maybe he'd like a bird. Maybe he'd enjoy a cat," said the shopkeeper.

Mortimer rolled his eyes. He slapped his forehead. "Don't you people know anything? I need a fish friend—like her!" Mortimer pointed to a cute little goldfish.

The goldfish smiled. She waved at Mortimer. Waldo bought the little fish, and Mortimer and Goldie lived happily ever after.

1. _____
2. _____
3. _____
4. _____
5. _____
6. _____
7. _____
8. _____
9. _____
10. _____

Name: _____   **Date:** _____

Another way to get rid of short, choppy sentences is to combine parts of two related sentences. If two sentences have the same predicate but different subjects, you can combine them to create a single sentence with a compound subject. As you know, a compound subject has two or more main words, joined by a connecting word.

CHOPPY: The walls were painted blue. The ceiling was painted blue.
SMOOTH: The walls and the ceiling were painted blue.

If two sentences have the same subject, you can create a sentence with a compound predicate by adding a comma and the words *and, but,* or *or* and removing the second subject.

CHOPPY: The painters scraped off the old paint. The painters filled in any cracks.
SMOOTH: The painters scraped off the old paint and filled in any cracks.

Directions: Write each pair of sentences as one sentence with a compound subject.

1. The old carpet is dirty. The old paint is dirty.

   _____

2. The walls must be cleaned. The floor must be cleaned.

   _____

3. Painters choose colors. Decorators choose colors.

   _____

4. The new paint looks good. The carpet looks good.

   _____

5. The carpet matches the walls. The couch matches the walls.

   _____

Directions: Write each pair of sentences as one sentence with a compound predicate.

6. Mr. and Mrs. Yasuda bought an old house. Mr. and Mrs. Yasuda fixed it up.

   _____

7. The house was pretty. The house needed some work.

   _____

8. The roof had a hole. The roof needed to be replaced.

   _____

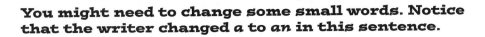

You might need to change some small words. Notice that the writer changed _a_ to _an_ in this sentence.

Another way to make your writing less choppy is to add the adjectives or adverbs from one sentence to another. These two sentences are both about a model airplane. You can combine them by moving the adjective _interesting_ to the first sentence.

    Alysha showed a model airplane to the class. The model was <u>interesting</u>.
    Alysha showed an <u>interesting</u> model airplane to the class.

The sentences below can be combined by moving the adverb _perfectly_.

    The model airplane could fly. It flew <u>perfectly</u>.
    The model airplane could fly <u>perfectly</u>.

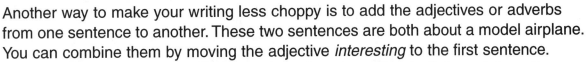

Directions: Combine each set of sentences by moving the underlined adjective or adverb to the first sentence.

1. Jordan had a model rocket. It was <u>huge</u>.

   _____

2. The rocket blasted off. It went <u>noisily</u>.

   _____

3. The rocket produced a lot of smoke. The smoke was <u>smelly</u>.

   _____

4. It soared into the sky. It soared <u>high</u>.

   _____

5. Everyone watched. Everyone watched <u>carefully</u>.

   _____

6. The parachute opened. It opened <u>too soon</u>.

   _____

7. The parachute did not do its job. The parachute was <u>faulty</u>.

   _____

8. The rocket came down. It came down <u>quickly</u>.

   _____

9. It crashed on the pavement. The pavement was <u>hard</u>.

   _____

10. The nose of the rocket was cracked. It was cracked <u>badly</u>.

   _____

Name: _____ **Date:** _____

It is important to avoid short, choppy sentences. However, it is also important to avoid long, stringy sentences. Stringy sentences are made up of two many sentences strung together with connecting words like and and so. They can be hard to read and can confuse the reader.

> STRINGY: I liked Jordan's rocket a lot and I wanted to learn more about rockets and I went to the library to get a book about it and then I decided to try making one of my own.

This sentence should be divided into two or three shorter sentences. There is more than one possible way to divide it.

> BETTER: I liked Jordan's rocket a lot. I wanted to learn more about rockets, so I went to the library to get a book about them. Then I decided to try making one of my own.

> BETTER: I liked Jordan's rocket a lot, and wanted to learn more about rockets. I went to the library to get a book about them, and then decided to try making one of my own.

Directions: Using your own paper, rewrite each stringy sentence.

1. Yesterday was really chilly and I was only wearing shorts and a T-shirt and so today I put on long pants and a sweater but now it's hot and sunny.

2. Usually the weather doesn't change so quickly but this spring it changes a lot and one minute it's chilly and the next minute it's warm.

3. It got warm for a few days in February and the leaves on the trees started to bud but then it suddenly got cold again and a lot of trees were hurt.

4. Very cold weather can damage some plants and so my mom and I always try to cover up our plants when we know the temperature is going to be below freezing.

5. We were able to save all of our plants last year by doing that and this year we thought we would be successful but then one night there was an ice storm that we didn't expect and so a lot of plants died.

Name: _____ **Date:** _____

Directions: Read the paragraph. Look for choppy sentences, stringy sentences, sentence fragments, and run-on sentences. Rewrite the paragraph, fixing any problems you find.

I am trying to learn to juggle. I'm trying hard. I saw some jugglers at a street fair last year and that got me interested in it and so I got a book at the library about juggling. The book makes it sound easy, it is not easy! First, you need to learn to catch. And throw two balls with one hand. It's tricky. It takes practice. I practiced every day for two weeks. Finally, I could toss and catch with one hand. I could toss and catch perfectly. Then it was time to add the third ball. What a disaster! I will have to keep practicing.

Name: _____   Date: _____

After you have chosen a topic for a paper, it is time to begin exploring the topic. You need to do this before you begin writing. When you explore a topic, you come up with ideas about it. You might use some of these ideas in your paper. There are many different prewriting activities you can do. Try some of the ones below.

Brainstorming: Quickly write a list of words and images about your topic.

<u>Hurricanes</u>

Lots of rain and wind
danger!

buildings can be damaged
you might have to leave the area

Clustering: Write your topic inside a circle. Think of words that are related to the topic. Write them quickly, circling each word. Group the words around your the central word.

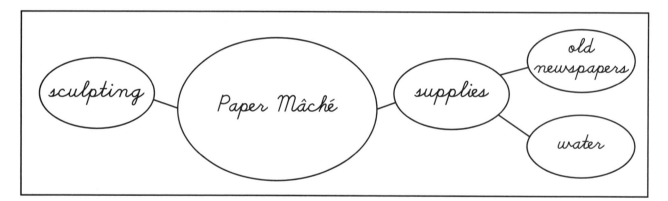

Asking Wh– Questions: Write *who?, what?, where?, how?,* and *why?* on a sheet of paper. Answer each question about your topic idea.

Who? Ben Franklin
What? inventor
Where? Philadelphia

Try these prewriting activities. You can use your ideas later to write a paragraph.

Directions: Think of a time that something scary happened to you. Answer the questions to come up with ideas for a paragraph you could write about it.

Who? _____

What? _____

When? _____

Where? _____

Why? _____

How? _____

Directions: What is your favorite food? Write ideas about it in a cluster diagram. Use as many circles, words, and groups of words as you like.

My Favorite Food

Once you begin exploring your topic, you may find that it is too big, or broad. There may be too much to say about it in a short paper. If this is the case, you will need to **narrow** your topic, or make it smaller. For example, the topic *Dinosaurs* may be too broad. There were many different kinds of dinosaurs. Each kind of dinosaur had its own habits and characteristics. Thousands of books and articles have been written about these creatures. Therefore, this topic is too broad to cover in a short paper. Therefore, the topic should be narrowed to something that you can write about easily in a short paper, such as *Dinosaur Myths, The Tiniest Dinosaur,* or *What Dinosaurs Ate.*

Directions: The topics below are too broad. Narrow the focus and write a narrow topic that would be appropriate for a short paper.

1. Broad Topic: Cars

   Narrow Topic: _____

2. Broad Topic: Music

   Narrow Topic: _____

3. Broad Topic: The ocean

   Narrow Topic: _____

4. Broad Topic: Horses

   Narrow Topic: _____

5. Broad Topic: Outerspace

   Narrow Topic: _____

Name: _____   **Date:** _____

Do not worry about spelling and handwriting when you take notes. Your notes are just for you!

Sometimes you need to do research on a topic before writing a report. Taking notes can help you remember important information that you read.

When you take notes, do not write down every word. Write only enough to help you remember the main ideas and most important facts. Put the information in your own words.

Your teacher might want to know where you found your information. Write down the titles, authors, and dates of the books, magazines, and other sources you use.

Read this paragraph and look at the notes Janice took. Janice wanted to find facts about Thomas Edison's early life.

> Thomas Edison was one of America's greatest inventors. He was born in Milan, Ohio in 1847. He was very intelligent, but he did not go to school. Instead, he was taught at home by his mother and a private teacher. Thomas also found time to work as a newsboy on the Grand Trunk Railroad. It was during this time that he started losing his hearing.

What was Thomas Edison's early life like?
— *born in Ohio, 1847*
— *intelligent*
— *taught at home*
— *worked as newsboy*
— *started losing hearing*

Directions: Read the paragraph. Take notes on the information to answer this question: What did Thomas Edison invent? Write your notes on the lines below. You do not need to write in complete sentences.

One of Edison's first inventions was a transmitter and receiver for the automatic telegraph machine. Later, he developed the telephone transmitter. He also invented the phonograph, which gave the world the very first recording of sound. Edison was fascinated with electricity, and this led him to create the first practical lightbulb in 1879. Later, he developed an electric railroad system. These are only a few of Edison's inventions. Altogether, he held over 1,000 patents.

What did Thomas Edison invent?

_____

_____

_____

_____

_____

_____

_____

_____

_____

_____

_____

_____

_____

_____

Name: _____   **Date:** _____

A good way to plan your writing is to make an outline. An outline is made up of main ideas and the details and facts that support them. Making an outline can help you decide what information to include in your paper. It can also help you organize your information and arrange it in a logical order.

Write a Roman numeral (I, II, III, IV) next to each main topic. The main topic will become the main idea of the paragraph when you write it. Write the subtopics underneath the main topic. The subtopics are the details that support the main idea. Start each subtopic with a capital letter.

Look at this outline Janice made from the notes she took about Thomas Edison's early life on page 115.

My Outline

I. Thomas Edison's early life
   A. Born in Ohio in 1847
   B. Intelligent
   C. Was taught at home
   D. Worked as a newsboy
   E. Started losing his hearing

Directions: Janice has taken the notes below. She has started making an outline for her paper. Finish the outline by filling in the blanks with information from her notes.

My Notes

What did Thomas Edison invent?
— transmitter and receiver for the automatic telegraph machine
— phonograph
— lightbulb
— electric railroad system

What else was Edison interested in?
— substitutes for rubber
— mining
— new uses for cement
— motion pictures

My Outline

II. Thomas Edison's inventions
   A. transmitter and receiver for the automatic telegraph machine
   B. _____
   C. _____
   D. electric railroad system

III. _____
   A. _____
   B. Mining
   C. _____
   D. motion pictures

Name: _____

Date: _____

A book report tells about a book you have read. It should give some information about the book and explain why you liked or disliked the book.

Begin a book report by telling the name of the book and the author's name. Then tell a little about the book. You might tell whether the book is sad, funny, or thrilling. Also tell who the main characters are. Next, tell a little about the plot of the story. You might tell what happens in one part of the story. However, do not give away any secrets! You don't want to spoil the ending for readers.

Finally, tell your opinion of the book. Did you like it? Why? Would you recommend this book? Why or why not?

Directions: Read the following book report and answer the questions.

Do you like exciting adventures? Then you will love <u>Under the Pacific Moon</u> by Eric Gillen. It's an exciting story about a Gregory and Clementine, a brother and sister who live on a ship. They sail around the world with their father, Captain Merriweather. Gregory and Clementine can't stay out of trouble! The most exciting part of the story was when the two children tried to climb up the mast. A big wave hit the ship, and Gregory fell into the water. Clementine had to save him from a shark. You'll be amazed to learn how she did it!

This book kept me on the edge of my seat the whole time. I also learned a lot about what it is like to live on a boat. If you like oceans and adventure, you will love this book, too.

1. What is the title of the book? _____

2. Who is the author? _____

3. Who are the main characters? _____

4. Is the book funny, sad, scary, or exciting? _____

5. Why did the writer like the book? _____

_____

_____

Name: _____   **Date:** _____

Directions: Think of a book or story you have read. Write a short book report about it. In your book report, be sure to include the title, the author's name, some information about the story, and your opinion.

_____

_____

_____

_____

_____

_____

_____

_____

_____

_____

_____

_____

_____

_____

_____

_____

_____

_____

_____

_____

_____

_____

Name: _____   **Date:** _____

An informational paragraph gives facts. A paragraph is a group of sentences that express one main idea. A paragraph has a topic sentence and supporting details. The **topic sentence** tells the main idea of the paragraph. It often comes at the beginning of the paragraph. The rest of the sentences in the paragraph give **supporting details** about the main idea. It is important to remember that each sentence must deal only with your topic and not mention other topics.

Directions: The paragraphs below contain information unrelated to the topic sentence. Underline the topic sentence in each paragraph. Cross out the unrelated information.

1. Not all prehistoric animals were dinosaurs. For example, wooly mammoths were huge mammals. I wish they were still alive today. They're cool. Some prehistoric animals were closely related to the dinosaurs, like the pterosaurs. I once saw their bones in a museum. Other animals, such as the shark and the giant turtle, lived at the same time some dinosaurs existed, but neither of these water animals are dinosaurs. I once had a pet turtle.

2. Santa Rosa Island, now called Pensacola Beach, Florida, is famous for being the first place where shots were fired in the Civil War. It happened on the evening of January 13, 1861, when the Confederate army commanded the Union army to give up control of Fort Pickens. My family visited the site last summer. The Union refused, and the first shot was fired outside the walls of Fort Pickens. The United States war sloop, Wyandotte, was anchored off the island. Florida has many small islands. 8,000 Confederate troops quickly moved into Pensacola, but they were not able to take Fort Pickens. Today Pensacola is a big town.

In an informational paragraph, the **supporting details** usually come in the sentences that follow the topic sentence. They give details about the main idea.

Read the paragraph. What details support the main idea?

> Making a company pay for polluting can sometimes make them stop. For example, in 2001, ABC Corporation was ordered to pay a two million dollar fine for dumping toxic sludge into the Harpoon River. The steep fine nearly put ABC out of business. Instead of quitting, however, the owner of ABC refocused his company's business. ABC Corporation now makes Earth-friendly soap suds. More and more people are buying their products now. ABC is off the "Pollution" list and on the "Green" list, thanks to a "fine" wake-up call.

In this paragraph, the writer supports her main idea, *Making a company pay for polluting can sometimes make them stop,* by explaining what happened when a particular company was fined for polluting a river.

An informational paragraph should have a **closing sentence** as well. The closing sentence repeats the main idea in a new way or makes a final comment about the details or main idea. What closing sentence did this writer use?

Directions: Write details that support the topic sentences. Write a closing sentence for each.

1. Topic Sentence: It is important to wear a helmet when you ride a bike or a skateboard.

   Supporting Details: _____

   _____

   _____

   Closing Sentence: _____

   _____

2. Topic Sentence: Dogs and monkeys can be trained to help people who have disabilities.

   Supporting Details: _____

   _____

   _____

   Closing Sentence: _____

   _____

Name: _____   **Date:** _____

Directions: Study the graph below and use the information to complete an informational paragraph. The topic sentence and closing sentence have been written for you.

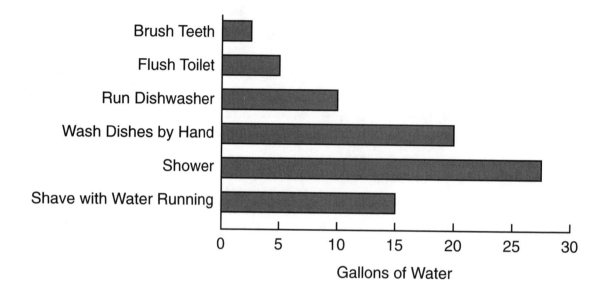

Average Daily Water Use Per Person

Gallons of Water

Most people use a lot of water every day. _____

_____

_____

_____

_____

_____

_____

_____

_____

_____

_____

Maybe everyone should find ways to conserve water.

Name: _____   Date: _____

You have learned that an informational paragraph begins with a topic sentence that states topic and main idea. The sentences that follow provide supporting details for the main idea. The paragraph ends with a closing sentence that wraps up the paragraph. An informational essay follows the same structure. The only difference is in the length.

An informational essay is made up of several paragraphs. The opening paragraph states topic and main idea. The paragraphs that follow provide supporting details for the main idea. The essay ends with a closing paragraph that wraps up the essay.

The paragraphs that provide supporting details, called the body paragraphs, each have their own topic sentence and supporting sentences. However, the main idea of each body paragraph supports the main idea of the whole essay. For example, the paragraph you wrote about average daily water use could be part of an essay on conserving resources.

An outline is an excellent way to organize and plan an informational essay. Complete this outline with your own ideas.

I. You can exercise anywhere.
    A. Exercising indoors
    B. Exercising outdoors

II. Exercises you can do indoors
    A. _____
    B. Dance
    C. _____

III. Exercises you can do outdoors
    A. Play basketball
    B. _____
    C. _____
    D. _____

IV. Closing Paragraph—You can exercise wherever you are.
    A. It is good for your health
    B. It can be fun

Name: _____ Date: _____

A **comparison and contrast** paper tells how two or more things are alike and how they are different. *Compare* means to show how things are alike. *Contrast* means to show differences. Like informational paragraphs, comparison and contrast paragraphs have a topic sentence and supporting details.

Read the following paragraphs. Which sentences are the topic sentences? Which sentences give supporting details?

Acoustic

Electric

Electric guitars and acoustic guitars are alike in many ways. They can both have either six or twelve strings. Both have a long neck and a body. They both have pegs at the top of the neck for tuning the strings. You can play both of them by strumming or plucking.

These two kinds of guitars have some differences, too. The body of an acoustic guitar is hollow. The body of an electric guitar is solid. The electric guitar has holes where you plug in the wires that lead to the amplifier. When you strum an acoustic guitar, the sound is loud. When you strum an electric guitar, the sound is soft until you plug it into the amplifier. Then it can be very loud.

Directions: How are an acoustic guitar and an electric guitar alike? How are they different? Fill in the chart with details from the paragraphs to show the similarities and differences.

ACOUSTIC ONLY	BOTH	ELECTRIC ONLY

Name: _____   **Date:** _____

The key to writing a successful comparison and contrast paper is organizing the details in a way that is clear and logical. One way to organize your details is to write one paragraph telling how the things being compared are alike. Then write another paragraph telling how they are different.

Directions: Tran took these notes on the similarities and differences between lions and tigers. He has started organizing them in a chart. Finish copying the notes in the chart, and then use them to write two paragraphs about lions and tigers. Write one paragraph comparing the two, and one contrasting the two.

My Notes

large
belong to the cat family
tan color
carnivores
expert hunters
orange and black stripes

Lions Only	Both	Tigers Only
live in Africa	_____	live all across Asia
live mostly in groups	_____	live mostly alone
_____	_____	_____
	_____	

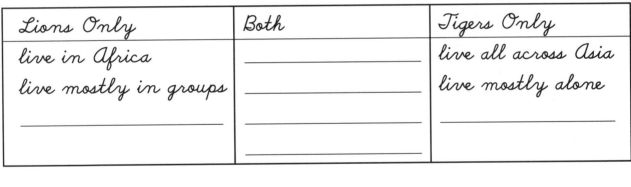

_____
_____
_____
_____
_____
_____
_____
_____
_____

Name: _____   **Date:** _____

A narrative paragraph tells a story about something that happened. It can be a true story or one you make up. A narrative paragraph might not have a topic sentence. However, it must have a main idea and details about the event.

The details must be given in an order, or sequence, that makes sense. Using order words such as *first, next, then, after, before, finally*, and *last* can help show the sequence of events.

Details can do more than tell the basic events. They can also make a story more interesting to read. Read these two paragraphs. Which paragraph holds your interest?

1. We were standing on the deck of the boat. Suddenly, a big gust of wind blew my hat off! It soared through the air and landed in the water with a splash. It bobbed up and down with the water. I started to lean over the railing to get it, but Captain Richards shouted at me to stop. I stared sadly as my cap started to drifted away. I was heartbroken.

2. Then my hat blew off. It fell in the water. I wanted to get it, but the man wouldn't let me.

The paragraphs tell about the same event, but the first one has details that make it more interesting. It tells where the event took place, how the writer felt, what the cap did, who the man was. These details help make the story more interesting.

Directions: Rewrite this story, adding details to make it more interesting. The details can answer *who, what, why, when, where,* or *how.*

I saw a letter in the mail box. I was curious. It was big. I got it out. It was for me. It was a card from my friend.

_____

_____

_____

_____

_____

_____

_____

_____

Name: _____ **Date:** _____

Another way to make a story more interesting is to use dialogue. When you use **dialogue**, you use the exact words of the speaker. Using dialogue can make your narrative seem more real and "alive."

Read the two paragraphs. Which one is more interesting and lively?

1. When I brought home my trophy, my mom said she was proud of me. My brother clapped and said I was the best chess player in the world. I laughed and told him that there were probably a few people around who could beat me. He smiled and shrugged and told me I was still number one in his book.

2. When I brought home my trophy, my mom said, "I'm so proud of you!"
    My brother clapped and said, "You're the best chess player in the world!"
    I laughed. "Well, there are probably a few people around who could beat me," I said.
    He smiled and shrugged, saying "You're still number one in my book."

The rules for writing dialogue are the same as for writing direct quotations:
- Put quotation marks around the speaker's exact words.
- Use a comma to set off phrases such as *said Amy* or *yelled Tom.*
- When one character stops speaking and another begins, start a new paragraph.

Directions: Rewrite this story, adding dialogue to make it more lively.

One day my dad brought home a scraggly little bush in a pot. He said it was a rose bush. I couldn't believe it. I told him there weren't any roses on it! He told me to wait until spring. Then I would see. I asked him where he got it. He said he found it on the curb. Someone was throwing it out. I told him I wasn't surprised they were throwing it away. It was ugly! But he just told me to grab a shovel and dig a hole. So I did. And wouldn't you know, this spring we had lovely roses in our yard!

_____

_____

_____

_____

_____

_____

_____

Name: _____   **Date:** _____

Directions: Write a story, true or made up, about one of the following topics. Remember to use details that tell *who, what, why, when, where,* or *how* and dialogue to make it lively and interesting.

TOPIC IDEAS

Having a cold
Losing something
Meeting a new friend

Name: _____   Date: _____

A descriptive paragraph describes a person, place, or thing. When you write a descriptive paragraph, you use words that help the reader imagine what you are writing about. Sense words can be used to paint a vivid picture of your topic. They can help you describe how something looks, sounds, smells, tastes, and feels.

The parrot <u>squawked</u> a greeting to the <u>fluffy</u>, <u>black</u> dog.

Which words help you "hear" the parrot? Which words help you "see" the dog?

Here are just a few sense words you can use.

Sight	Sound	Touch	Taste	Smell
shiny	roar	slick	tart	smoky
dazzling	snap	downy	sweet	minty
shady	whimper	prickly	syrupy	sweet
orange	shriek	smooth	salty	rotten

Directions: This paragraph describes the scene in the woods. What sensory details does the writer include? Fill in senses chart with details from the paragraph.

The woods near my house seem peaceful, but they're really full of activity. As I sit on the soft blanket of pine needles under my favorite tree, I can hear a squirrel chattering angrily at a screeching bluejay. I bend down to look at a mossy, hollow log, and see tiny black ants marching to and fro. The tree oozes sticky sap. It has a sharp, piney smell. It tastes sweet to the ants, and they nibble at the dried crystals of sap.

LOOK	FEEL	SMELL	TASTE	SOUND

Name: _____   Date: _____

The right words can make a sentence come alive for a reader. Exact nouns, descriptive adjectives and adverbs, and figurative language can all be used to paint a clear picture. Read these pairs of sentences.

The <u>car</u> <u>stopped suddenly</u>.
The <u>red convertible</u> <u>screeched to a halt</u>.

The <u>ice cream</u> was <u>good</u>.
The <u>banana-walnut ice cream</u> was <u>fruity and crunchy</u>.

The <u>dress</u> was made of <u>nice fabric</u>.
The <u>ballgown</u> was made of the <u>finest pink velvet</u>.

The first sentence of each pair states only the bare facts. It does not paint a vivid picture for the reader. The second sentence of each pair uses exact words that give the reader a clear picture. They describe things more fully and are more interesting to read.

Directions: Rewrite each sentence, changing the underlined words to more descriptive ones. If you want to, you may also change the other words.

1. Dad brought home a <u>nice plant</u>.

_____

2. The <u>food</u> smells <u>good</u>.

_____

3. <u>The children</u> are <u>making noise</u>.

_____

4. <u>My pet</u> is <u>nice</u>.

_____

5. <u>The man</u> wore a <u>colorful</u> shirt.

_____

6. <u>The game</u> was <u>enjoyable</u>.

_____

7. My head <u>hurts</u>.

_____

8. Emmanuel saw a <u>good</u> movie.

_____

9. I felt <u>bad</u> after eating the <u>food</u>.

_____

Name: _____   **Date:** _____

Directions: Write a paragraph describing someplace in your school, such as a playground, a lunchroom, or a classroom. You may use the senses chart to plan details.

LOOK	FEEL	SMELL	TASTE	SOUND

_____

_____

_____

_____

_____

_____

_____

_____

_____

_____

_____

_____

_____

_____

_____

Name: _____   **Date:** _____

When you write a persuasive paragraph, you try to persuade the reader to do or agree with your opinion. This is done by stating your purpose, or what you want the reader to do. This should be done in the topic sentence of the paragraph. Next, you must persuade the reader to do it. This is done by giving strong reasons. Facts and examples can make the your reasons stronger.

Prewriting activities can help you think of strong reasons. First, turn your purpose into a "why" question. Then think of several "because" answers. The strongest answers can be the reasons in your paragraph.

Shawn has started planning a persuasive letter to his science teacher. Which of his reasons is the strongest? Which is the weakest?

> My purpose: Our class should take a trip to the science museum.
> Why question: Why should our class take a trip to the science museum?
> Answer: Because we are studying the planets, and there is a good exhibit on the planets there.
> Answer: Because my sister works there, so I could see her.
> Answer: Because we could learn about other things at the museum.
> Answer: Because some students have never been there before, and the trip would give them a chance to see it.

Directions: Think of an activity you would like your class to do. Do this prewriting exercise to plan a persuasive paragraph for your teacher. First, write a "why" question for your purpose. Then write "because" answers for your reasons. You will use the ideas you write here to write a paragraph later.

My purpose: _____

_____

Why question: _____

_____

Answer: _____

_____

Answer: _____

_____

Answer: _____

_____

Answer: _____

_____

Name: _____   Date: _____

Your purpose needs strong support to persuade the reader. Examples and facts give strong support. Facts can be proved. Opinions make weak support. Opinions tell what someone thinks or believes. They cannot be proved. If the reader disagrees with the opinions you use as support, he or she will probably not be persuaded to agree with your purpose.

Purpose: Our class should collect cans for recycling.
Weak Support: It's a good thing to do.
Strong Support: Recycling can reduce the waste that goes into the garbage.

Directions: Read the purposes and reasons below. Replace the weak support with a strong fact or example.

1. Purpose: Our class should have a pet lizard.

   Weak Support: I'll be the best babysitter ever!

   Strong Support: _____

   _____

2. Purpose: Our class should have a picnic at Foster Park.

   Weak Support: I'll be the best babysitter ever!

   Strong Support: _____

   _____

Name: _____   **Date:** _____

Directions: Use the purpose and reasons you come up with on page 133 to write a persuasive paragraph. Remember to begin by stating your purpose. Support your reasons with facts and examples.

_____

_____

_____

_____

_____

_____

_____

_____

_____

_____

_____

_____

_____

_____

_____

_____

_____

_____

_____

_____

_____

_____

_____

_____

_____

Name: _____   **Date:** _____

SUMMARIZING

A **summary** is a short version of a longer passage. A summary contains the main ideas and important details of the passage. Writing a summary is similar to taking notes, which you practiced on pages 115–116 of this workbook. However, a summary is written in complete sentences and in the form of a paragraph. Read this paragraph, and then study the summary of it that follows.

Have you ever wondered where certain kinds of dinosaurs get their names? Dinosaurs are usually named by the scientists who discover them. A new dinosaur may be given a name based on a certain characteristic it has—large eyes, small feet, a long tail. The dinosaur may also be named after the place where the bones were discovered, or they may be named in honor of the wealthy person who helped pay for the scientist's research.

Summary

Scientists have several methods of naming a new dinosaur. They might give it a name based on a characteristic, the place it was found, or the person who paid for the research.

The main idea of the longer paragraph is that scientists can choose a name in several ways. This idea becomes the topic sentence of the summary. The second sentence of the summary gives the most important details about the ways scientists choose the names.

When you write a summary, remember to state the main idea of the passage in the topic sentence, include only the most important points, and write the summary in your own words.

Directions: Read the two paragraphs about acoustic guitars and electric guitars on page 124 of this workbook. Write a short summary of them on the lines below.

_____
_____
_____
_____
_____

Name: _____ Date: _____

The last step when doing any kind of writing is to proofread your work. When you proofread, you look for errors, such as incomplete sentences, punctuation errors, and spelling errors. When you proofread, check for one kind of error at a time. A checklist can be helpful when you proofread.

Proofreading Checklist

❏ **Are there incomplete sentences or run-on sentences?**

❏ **Does each sentence begin with a capital letter and end with the correct end mark?**

❏ **Are apostrophes used correctly?**

❏ **Do subjects and verbs agree?**

❏ **Are words spelled correctly?**

Directions: Proofread this letter. Use the checklist. Write the new letter on the lines below.

Dear Alyssa,

How would you like a visitor? My mother has a business meeting in chicago next month. And said I can join her for the week. If your parents say it's OK, I can hang out with you during the day while my mom is at her meetings. wouldn't that be great?

I was in Chicago once when I was a baby, I do not remember anything about the trip. Im excited to see the city again! My mom says Chicago is a fun city. We can go to a muzeum or just hang out and play. Let me know what your parents says. I cant wait to see you!

Love,
Marisol

_____

_____

_____

_____

_____

_____

_____

_____

_____

Name: _____   **Date:** _____

PAGE 6
1. Jesse Owens
2. Lisa Lewis
3. David Chung
4. Maria Lopez
5. Eric Wilson
6. Jerry and Linda
7. Lucinda and Andre Baxter
8. Christa Fleming.
9. Bryan, Casey Fletcher.
10. Amy Solomon and Shaun Ryder

PAGE 7
1. Mr. Mackey
2. Dr. Sanderson
3. Governor Hawkins
4. Miss Lanier
5. Aunt Marion
6. Ms. Smith
7. Dr. Mack's
8. President Eisenhower
9. Grandma's
10. Mr. Geller, Uncle Juán

PAGE 8
Max, Pepper
Lady, Buddy
Bear, Brandy
Smokey, Ginger
Shadow, Missy
Naming pets—Answers will vary, but each will have an initial capital letter.

PAGE 9
1. London, England
2. Hollywood, California
3. Oakland Avenue
4. Japan
5. Herrin, Illinois
6. [name of state, first letter(s) capitalized]
7. [name of a street, first letter(s) capitalized]
8. [name of country, first letter(s) capitalized]
9. [name of state, first letter(s) capitalized]
10. Rhode Island

PAGE 10
1. Glacier National Park
2. the Sears Tower
3. the Mississippi River
4. the Astrodome
5. Pike's Peak
6. Museum, Science
7. Wrigley, Field, Chicago
8. Colorado, River, Austin, Texas
9. Alps, France
10. Lake, Ontario

PAGE 11
1. Saturday, June 29
2. December 19
3. Thursday, May 27
4. April 17
5. Monday and Tuesday
6. [month]
7. Monday, Friday
8. January
9. December
10. Answers will vary.

PAGE 12
1. Memorial Day
2. April Fool's Day
3. Groundhog Day
4. Columbus Day
5. Earth Day
6. Kwanza
7. Labor Day
8. Grandparents' Day, Mother's Day
9. Valentine's Day
10. Easter, Passover

PAGE 13
1. the Dallas Cowboys
2. Glendale Drama Club
3. Winkler School
4. the Red Cross
5. Freshplus Grocery Store
6. Dazzle Hair Salon
7. Spanish, English
8. Hindu
9. Green Bay Packers
10. American Cancer Society

PAGE 14
1. National Velvet
2. Highlights
3. the Harrisburg Herald
4. National Geographic
5. The Wizard of Oz
6. The movie, Seabiscuit, is based on a true story.
7. Jackie reads the Seattle Sentinel every morning.
8. Have you read Ali Baba and the Forty Thieves?
9. My baby brother's favorite book is Pat the Bunny.
10. Maya reads Critters Magazine every month.

PAGE 15
1. Lawrence hopped out of the car.
2. The wind mussed his hair. He ran to the water's edge.
3. Mom and Aunt Kathy followed with the picnic basket.
4. Lawrence let the water lap at his toes. It was chilly.
5. Mom called to him. He ran to help carry the folding chairs.
6. Aunt Kathy opened the big beach umbrella. She stuck it in the sand.
7. Lawrence helped Mom spread out the big blanket.
8. Then, they all splashed into the water.
9. They had a wonderful time at the beach.

PAGE 16
Burnet Drive
Freeport, California
August
Dear Aunt Carol
Thank
I
Now I
The
Monica
I
We
We
Freeport
School of Art, Both
Please, We
Love,
Ian

PAGE 17
1. Lorenzo went to Madrid to visit his Uncle Felipe last July.
2. It was his first trip to Spain.
3. The airplane crossed the Atlantic Ocean.
4. Uncle Felipe had many activities planned.
5. He took Lorenzo to the Prado, a famous museum.
6. There were several paintings by Pablo Picasso.
7. Later, they went to a movie theater to see Toy Story in Spanish.
8. Lorenzo liked playing with Uncle Felipe's dog Rosita.
9. After two weeks, it was time to fly back to Minnesota.
10. Next Thanksgiving, Uncle Felipe will come to visit.

PAGE 18
1. .
2. ?
3. .
4. .
5. ?
6. .
7. ?
8. .
9. .
10. ?

PAGE 19
1. !
2. .
3. !
4. !
5. .
6. !
7. .
8. !
9. .
10. ! or .
11. .
12. !
13. .
14. !
15. .

PAGE 20
1. .
2. ?
3. !
4. .
5. .
6. ?
7. .
8. !
9. ?
10. ! or .
11. .
12. .
13. ?
14. .
15. !

PAGE 21
1. Oscar's
2. sheep's
3. candle's
4. computer's
5. horses'
6. Farley's
7. oxen's
8. plant's
9. Dr. Seuss's
10. men's

PAGE 22
1. was not
2. do not
3. could not
4. should not
5. had not
6. hasn't
7. wouldn't
8. aren't
9. won't
10. isn't

PAGE 23
1. She's
2. It's
3. They've
4. It'll
5. You've
6. He's
7. We're
8. They're
9. They've
10. It'll

PAGE 24
1. My hobbies are reading, drawing, and playing basketball.
2. The new uniforms are blue, white, and green.
3. We wear long pants, white shirts, and blue ties.
4. Mickey, Robert, Julie, and Ashley worked on their project.
5. Playing tag, jumping rope, and dancing are fun ways to exercise.
6.–10. Answers will vary.

PAGE 25
1. Greg,
2. Yes, … week,
3. Well,
4. Yes,
5. about,
6. Well,
7. yourself,
8.–10. Answers will vary.

PAGE 26
1. small, but it is
2. wants, and they have a good life there.
3. situations, or they were
4. pets, but the owners
5. circus, and the tiger
6. beautiful, but they
7. free, but it is
8. money, or you
9. fruit, and they
10. once, and the zoo

PAGE 27
1. March 4, 1966
2. April 17, 1935
3. December 12, 2003
4. February 21, 1844
5. July 1, 2001
6. January 17, 1999
7. September 8, 2005
8. November 15, 1987
9. June 24, 1866
10. October 10, 1785

PAGE 28
1. 4072 Gleane St. Elmhurst, NY 11373
2. 4754 Francisco Dr. Pensacola, FL 32504
3. 862 Illinois Ave. Chicago, IL 60609
4. 29 Compo Road Westport, CT 06880
5. 1224 Bob Herman Rd. Atlanta, GA 31408
6. Athens,
7. Casablanca,
8. Monterrey,
9. Reykjavik,
10. Bydgoszcz,

PAGE 29
1. Gina, Shannon, and Courtney wrote a play together.
2. I read it, and it is pretty good.
3. Holly won't be old enough to vote until May 15, 2015.
4. Alexandria, Egypt, is an ancient city.
5. Yes, Josh, you can have a snack.
6. First, go wash your hands.
7. I will slice an apple for you, or you can eat a banana.
8. The students wrote reports, made posters, and gave speeches about air pollution.
9. Tomorrow, Mr. Hawkins, I will come on time.
10. Mr. Hawkins gave us instructions for the project.
11. First, we must gather the materials.
12. We will need posters, paper, markers, scissors, and glue.
13. We use the markers to draw, decorate, and number each shape.
14. Next, we need to cut out the shapes and glue them on the poster.
15. Finally, we need to let the glue dry for several hours.

PAGE 30
1. Nov.
2. Tues.
3. Dec.
4. Thurs.
5. Apr.
6. Wed.
7. Oct.
8. Mon.
9. Feb.
10. Sun.

PAGE 31
1. Ms. Rosen
2. Dr. Thomas
3. Allen Hastings, Sr.
4. Miss Elliot
5. Mrs. Haverty
6. Dr. ... Rd.
7. Jr. ... Blvd.
8. Mr. ... Ave.
9. Co. ... P.O.
10. Sr. ... St.

PAGE 32
1. Victor asked, "Where are my keys?"
2. "You are always late!" Cody complained.
3. "I'll be there," assured Sam.
4. Marie cried, "Look out for that swarm of bees!"
5. "I'll see you in six months," said the hygienist.
6. "I'll never tell your secret," she promised.
7. "Your voice is so loud!" scolded Ms. Jones.
8. "Give me liberty or give me death," declared Patrick Henry.
9. "Dave lost my book!" moaned Todd.
10. "Put things back where you found them," instructed my teacher.

PAGE 33
1. The teacher asked, "Who knows this story?"
2. Lisa cried, "That's one of my favorites!"
3. Ethan sighed, "It always rains on Saturday."
4. Mr. Morton called, "Who wants to go for a drive?"
5. Andre wondered, "How do they change the bulbs on the radio towers?"
6. Mom shouted, "Get in here right now, Montel!"
7. Kimberly replied, "No, that's not my hat."
8. Gordon exclaimed, "Now I've seen it all!"
9. Nellie whispered, "You're stepping on my foot, Brandon."
10. Anson suggested, "Wash it, and put a bandage on it."

PAGE 34
1. "I'll drive you home now," said Mrs. Johnson.
2. "What a huge stadium!" cried Matthew.
3. "What do bears do in the winter?" asked Sherman.
4. "They hibernate," answered Jake.
5. "Go brush your teeth!" ordered Mom.
6. "Will you help me with my math problems?" asked Drew.
7. "Can hummingbirds really fly backwards?" wondered Kathryn.
8. "Yes, they sure can," I replied.
9. "What a mess you've made!" exclaimed Tabitha.
10. "What color paint did you choose?" asked Molly.

PAGE 35
1. "Always and Forever" was my parents' wedding song.
2. Have you ever read the short story, "The Boar Pig," by Saki?
3. My dad's favorite poem is "If," by Rudyard Kipling.
4. Hetta read a poem called "If I Could."
5. The crowd sang "Take Me Out to the Ballgame" together.
6. My little brother loves to sing "Old McDonald" over and over.
7. "The Star Spangled Banner" is often sung at sporting events.
8. Graham read a scary story called "The Locked Door."
9. The short story, "Tiny Dancer," was made into a movie.
10. "Who Ordered the Broiled Face?" is a silly poem by Shel Silverstein.

PAGE 36
1. (they moved in last week)
2. (one hour from now)
3. (on the grill)
4. (I'm a vegetarian)
5. (my favorite kind)
6. (dusting and vacuuming)
7. (the ones with the red flowers)
8. (I'm 8, and Grayson is 11)
9. (the boys)
10. (soccer and reading)

PAGE 37
1. Dr. Karnes isn't at work today.
2. What did you do today?
3. I'm not allergic to cats.
4. Please bring a pen, some paper, and a ruler to class.
5. Huckleberry Finn is my favorite book.
6. "I am so happy you called!" cried Aunt Donna.
7. Is this Gary's backpack?
8. First, we need set a date for the party.
9. Maxine was born March 28, 1998 in Norman, Oklahoma.
10. Jack is tall, but the giant is taller.

PAGE 38
Drew thrilled the audience with her performance.
The lifeguard patrolled the beach in a red jeep.
I sent the invitations over a week ago.
The man with the blue jacket is my neighbor.

PAGE 39
Subjects are underlined; the not-underlined words are the predicates.
1. The pitcher practiced his fastball until he got it perfect.
2. The chef prepared a tasty stew.
3. Bert tripped on the rug.
4. The concerts usually last about an hour.
5. Mr. and Mrs. Trimble keep their garden tidy.
6. The huge grizzly bear yawned lazily.
7. Robin answered the phone.
8. Frankie played a joke on his little sister.
9. I enjoy playing kickball.
10. Ian's friend Barry came over.

PAGE 40
1. The <u>knight</u> was afraid of nothing.
2. All the other <u>knights</u> admired him.
3. <u>He</u> was known for his bravery.
4. The <u>king</u> rewarded the knight's bravery.
5. The <u>princess</u> married the gallant knight.
6.–10. Answers will vary.

PAGE 41
1. <u>practices</u>
2. <u>popped</u>
3. <u>drinks</u>
4. <u>arrived</u>
5. <u>melted</u>
6. <u>snapped</u>
7. <u>looks</u>
8. <u>wants</u>
9. <u>floated</u>
10. <u>lasted</u>

PAGE 42
1. Bill went to Justin's house, but Justin wasn't home.
2. The concert is free, but you have to pay to park.
3. The fireworks were fantastic, and we wanted them to last all night.
4. You fold the napkins, and I'll iron the tablecloth.
5. Would you like to play a game, or would you rather do a puzzle?
6.–10. Answers will vary.

PAGE 43
Sentences 1, 3, 5, 8, and 10 have compound subjects.

PAGE 44
Sentences 1, 3, 5, 7, 9, and 10 have compound predicates.

PAGE 45
1.–5. Answers will vary.
Persons: customers, Chef Pierre, waiters, George, Treena
Places: restaurant, Rooterville
Things: door, pizza, trays, dishes, lips, article, newspaper

PAGE 46
Answers will vary.
1. cousin, <u>California</u>
2. dog, <u>Rufus</u>
3. teachers, <u>Brush School</u>
4. stars, <u>Big Dipper</u>
5. <u>Hawaii</u>, islands

PAGE 47
1. boxes
2. drums
3. recesses
4. brushes
5. chairs
6. puzzles
7. eyelashes
8. peaches
9. hosts
10. bowls
11. plates
12. boxes
13. spots
14. ears
15. sandwiches

PAGE 48
1. ladies
2. birthdays
3. puppies
4. keys
5. toys
6. rubies
7. hobbies
8. flies
9. ferries
10. bodies
11. stories
12. libraries
13. alleys
14. fireflies
15. bluejays

PAGE 49
1. teeth
2. geese
3. sheep
4. oxen
5. moose
6. plural
7. singular
8. plural
9. plural
10. singular

PAGE 50
1. companies
2. notebooks
3. batches
4. mice
5. radishes
6. sheep
7. tables
8. feet
9. circuses
10. parties
11. children
12. ponies
13. holidays
14. plants
15. flies
16. wishes
17. daisies
18. tulips
19. teeth
20. lunches

PAGE 51
1. Brad's
2. dog's
3. uncle's
4. friend's
5. singer's
6. Tess's
7. lion's
8. passenger's
9. sister's
10. broom's

PAGE 52
1. friends'
2. moose's
3. cows'
4. women's
5. factories'
6. geese's
7. pioneers'
8. guests'
9. mice's
10. knights'

PAGE 53
1. friends'
2. girl's
3. principal's
4. brothers'
5. sisters'
6. book's
7. story's
8. children's
9. theater's
10. students'

PAGE 54
1. Mr. Walters, He
2. Christopher and Molly, They
3. statue, it
4. Jack, him
5. puddle, It
6. girls, them
7. shoes, them
8. Leah, her
9. antelope, it
10. chips, they

PAGE 55
1. We
2. They
3. We
4. She
5. They
My friends and <u>I</u> climbed aboard the airplane. This was our first trip on an airplane, and <u>we</u> were very excited. The plane rolled down the runway. Then <u>it</u> rose into the air! <u>It</u> was very noisy. Later, the flight attendant came by. <u>He</u> offered drinks and snacks. <u>I</u> was too excited to eat anything, but my friends were not. <u>They</u> got juice and pretzels.

PAGE 56
1. them
2. it
3. us
4. him
5. them
6. it
7. us
8. her
9. it
10. them

PAGE 57
1. I
2. me
3. me
4. me
5. I
6. I
7. me
8. I
9. me
10. I

PAGE 58
1. Our
2. its
3. my
4. your
5. her
6. his
7. its
8. their
9. its
10. her

PAGE 59
I, my, it, we, them
1. They
2. us
3. their
4. her
5. her

PAGE 60
1. stomp
2. sleep
3. chases
4. chews
5. yells
6. <u>goes</u> to the lumber yard.
7. <u>buys</u> a big stack of boards.
8. <u>measures</u> each board.
9. <u>cuts</u> the boards with an electric saw.
10. Together … <u>build</u> a fence to keep the dogs out.

PAGE 61
1. <u>has</u> finished
2. <u>are</u> going
3. <u>were</u> wearing
4. <u>had</u> read
5. <u>has</u> faded
6. <u>has</u> fallen
7. <u>will</u> become
8. <u>are</u> held
9. <u>is</u> flashing
10. <u>am</u> playing

PAGE 62
1. stands
2. buy
3. takes
4. stare
5. prance
6. wears
7. rides
8. swing
9. pedals
10. ride
11. laughs and cheers

PAGE 63
1. puts
2. sew
3. make
4. sprays
5. use
6. greet or rest
7. talks, solves, or observes
8. greet or rest
9. talks, solves, or observes
10. talks, solves, or observes

PAGE 64
1. watches
2. mixes
3. reaches

4. dries
5. carries
6. misses
7. rushes
8. flies
9. pushes
10. buzzes

PAGE 65
1. drives
2. passes
3. practice
4. fixes
5. wish
6. wear
7. wants
8. help
9. scurry
10. teaches

PAGE 66
1. will call
2. will clean
3. will recognize
4. will return
5. will announce
6.–10. Answers will vary.

PAGE 67
1. stopped
2. hopped
3. obeyed
4. glued
5. colored
6. tidied
7. tickled
8. married
9. sprayed
10. hoped
11. The ink smeared on the paper.
12. The river supplied the town with water.
13. The dogs begged for a piece of bacon.
14. Those wolves howled at the moon all night.
15. Uncle Peter baked the pumpkin pie.

PAGE 68
1. strolled
2. slipped
3. spilled
4. stomped
5. grabbed
6. wiped
7. spied
8. hurried
9. tripped, scraped
10. sighed, limped

PAGE 69
1. had ripped
2. have stayed
3. has started
4. had packed
5. has rained
6. has changed
7. has opened
8. have sprouted
9. have carried
10. have trimmed

PAGE 70
1. flown
2. knew
3. thrown
4. grew
5. threw
6. flown
7. known
8. grew
9. flew
10. grown

PAGE 71
1. begun
2. broken
3. began
4. worn
5. worn
6. wore
7. brought
8. worn
9. broke
10. wore

PAGE 72
1. found
2. told
3. found
4. said
5. said
6. made
7. told
8. made
9. told
10. made

PAGE 73
1. is
2. were
3. is
4. were
5. is
6. are
7. are
8. was
9. were
10. am

PAGE 74
1. interesting
2. shiny green
3. some
4. long
5. several
6. Two → students
7. strange → insects
8. long & thin → bodies
9. stinky → odor
10. new → leg

PAGE 75
1. gloomy, weather
2. gray, sky
3. wet, shoes
4. chilly, She
5. cheerful, fireplace
6. cozy, armchair
7. warm, feet
8. sleepy, She
9. heavy, eyelids
10. sweet, dreams

PAGE 76
1. an
2. an
3. the
4. a
5. the
6. the
7. a
8. a
9. the
10. an
11. A
12. A
13. the
14. the
15. a

PAGE 77
1. nicest
2. smaller
3. brighter
4. thicker
5. easiest
6. wider
7. widest
8. drier
9. harder
10. funniest

PAGE 78
1. floppiest
2. hotter
3. wiser
4. chewier
5. safest
6. prettiest
7. thinner
8. friendlier
9. softer
10. saddest

PAGE 79
1. most
2. most
3. more
4. most
5. more
6. most interesting
7. more unusual
8. most graceful
9. more flexible
10. more intelligent

PAGE 80
1. worst
2. worse
3. better
4. worse
5. better
6. best
7. worst
8. better
9. best
10. better

PAGE 81
1. sore → toe
2. hot → sun
3. important → speech
4. wonderful → present
5. deep → mud
6. most confident
7. tiniest
8. stranger
9. better
10. worst

PAGE 82
1. finally, when
2. nearby, where
3. always, when
4. carefully, how
5. Sometimes, how
6. once, lived
7. there, worked
8. always, had
9. usually, milked
10. easily, carried

PAGE 83
1. more sweetly
2. lower
3. more gently
4. highest
5. harder
6. most loudly
7. faster
8. more slowly
9. longer
10. more carefully

PAGE 84
1. good
2. well
3. well
4. good
5. well
6. well
7. well
8. good
9. good
10. well

PAGE 85
1. more neatly
2. faster
3. most creatively
4. more skillfully
5. hardest
6. good
7. well
8. good
9. good
10. well

PAGE 86
1. any
2. ever
3. any
4. ever
5. anybody
6. anywhere
7. any
8. ever
9. anyone
10. any

PAGE 87
1. reopen
2. overwork
3. disrespect
4. overdo
5. disapprove
6. rewrite
7. overheated
8. disobeyed
9. overload
10. dishonest

PAGE 88
1. viewable
2. painful
3. avoidable
4. understandable
5. hairless
6. fearful
7. repairable
8. useless
9. helpful
10. playable

PAGE 89
1. It's
2. They're
3. your
4. Their
5. their
6. its
7. there
8. You're
9. It's
10. your

PAGE 90
Answers will vary.

PAGE 91
1. already, all ready
2. lie, lay
3. good, well
4. leave, let
5. Set, sit

PAGE 92
Answers will vary.
Sample answers:

1. newspaper, newsboy, newsgirl, newsletter
2. sundown, sunset
3. starship, starlight
4. eyebrow, eyeliner
5. handcart, handbill, handclasp, handcuff
6. somebody, someday, someone, something
7. everybody, everyday, everyone, everywhere
8. playact, playbill, playback, playhouse, playland
9. thumbnail, thumbscrew, thumbtack
10. lipreader, lipstick

PAGE 93
1. b
2. a
3. b
4. c
5. c
6. b
7. b
8. b
9. a
10. c

PAGE 94
1. under
2. soft, easy
3. smooth
4. straight, honest
5. careless
6. cheerfully
7. noisy
8. messy
9. enjoys
10. foolish

PAGE 95
1. figurative
2. literal
3. literal
4. figurative
5. figurative
6.–10. Answers will vary.

PAGE 96
1. simile
2. metaphor
3. simile
4. metaphor
5. metaphor
6.–10. Answers will vary.

PAGE 97
Second part of each question will vary.
1. winter wind
2. teapot
3. camera
4. cake
5. tears

PAGE 98
1. plot
2. pluck
3. **1.** To break up soil with a plow.
4. **2.** The series of events in a play or story.
5. **1.** To detach by holding and pulling with the fingers; pick: pluck a flower.

PAGE 99
1. severe, serious
2. rotten, spoiled
3. evil, wicked
4. naughty, disobedient
5. sorry, regretful, sad
6. unappetizing
7. harmful, damaging
8. defective
9. sad
10. sick, ill

PAGE 100
1. 2 (bat)
2. 6 (fish), 17 (sleep)
3. 5 (Edison), 11 (light bulb)
4. 10 (Japan), 6 (flags)
5. 5 (engines), 7 (gas engines), 17 (steam engines)

PAGE 101
1. Chapter 3
2. Chapter 1
3. Chapter 3
4. page 4
5. page 11
6. 3 pages
7. Chapter 2
8. Chapter 3
9. Chapter 6
10. Chapter 5

PAGE 102
1. 58
2. 26
3. 49–50
4. 25, 32
5. 27
6. 3
7. 2
8. 5
9. 5–6
10. 6

PAGE 103
1. Hummingbirds have thin beaks and long, thin tongues.
2. They fly to a flower, then sip the nectar.
3. They lap it up with their long tongues.
4. They have tiny wings that beat hundreds of times per minute.
5. They have to eat a lot because of the amount of energy they burn.
6. They sip at the flowers while hovering in one place.
7. I saw one yesterday by the honeysuckle bush.
8. You can really hear a humming noise from their beating wings.
9. Hummingbirds are tiny, but very fierce.
10. They will defend their area from other birds.

PAGE 104
1. The two goats longed to eat the grass on the other side of the river.
2. He was mean and yelled a lot.
3. He was six feet tall with long, sharp horns.
4. Thor just laughed and stomped his feet.
5. Then Thor scooped up the troll with his steely horns.

PAGE 105
1. I love raccoons. They are my favorite animal.
2. Their faces are so cute. They look like they're wearing a mask.
3. Their tails are bushy. They have rings.
4. You have probably seen one because they live everywhere.
5. They can live in the forest and they can live in towns.
6. Sometimes they cause trouble when they open garbage cans.
7. They will eat almost anything. They will even eat food scraps.
8. They like to eat fish and crawdads, and they love berries and sweet corn.
9. They have a funny habit. They often dip their food in water before eating.
10. Be careful if you see a sick raccoon because it may have rabies.

PAGE 106
My favorite singer is David Winslow. <u>He has a great voice, and his songs are beautiful.</u> My sister is so lucky. She got to meet him last week! <u>She works at a restaurant where she is a waitress.</u> Well, one day last week David Winslow came to eat there. My sister waited on him. <u>She said she got very nervous. Her hands were shaking.</u> He ordered spaghetti. My sister was so nervous that she forgot to bring him a fork! <u>He was nice. He didn't get mad.</u> But then she spilled water on him. <u>She was very embarrassed, but he still wasn't angry.</u> He even gave her his autograph.

PAGE 107
1. Waldo sat by Mortimer's bowl, and he looked at the guppy.
2. The guppy sighed, and a tear rolled down his cheek.
3. Mortimer was lonely, and he needed a friend.
4. Waldo picked up the fish bowl, and they went to the pet store.
5. The shopkeeper smiled, and he greeted them.
6. The shopkeeper had an idea, but it was not a good one.
7. Waldo frowned, and he shook his head.
8. Maybe he'd like a bird, or maybe he'd enjoy a cat.
9. Mortimer rolled his eyes, and he slapped his forehead.
10. The goldfish smiled, and she waved at Mortimer.

PAGE 108
1. The old carpet and paint are dirty.
2. The walls and floor must be cleaned.
3. Painters and decorators choose colors.
4. The new paint and carpet look good.
5. The carpet and couch match the walls.
6. Mr. and Mrs. Yasuda bought an old house and fixed it up.
7. The house was pretty but needed some work.
8. The roof had a hole and needed to be replaced.

PAGE 109
1. Jordan had a <u>huge</u> model rocket.
2. The rocket blasted off <u>noisily</u>.
3. The rocket produced a lot of <u>smelly</u> smoke.
4. It soared <u>high</u> into the sky.
5. Everyone watched <u>carefully</u>.
6. The parachute opened <u>too soon</u>.
7. The <u>faulty</u> parachute did not do its job.
8. The rocket came down <u>quickly</u>.
9. It crashed on the <u>hard</u> pavement.
10. The nose of the rocket was <u>badly</u> cracked.

PAGE 110
1. Yesterday was really chilly. I was only wearing shorts and a T-shirt. So, today I put on long pants and a sweater. Now it's hot and sunny.
2. Usually the weather doesn't change so

quickly. But this spring, it changes a lot. One minute it's chilly, and the next minute it's warm.

3. It got warm for a few days in February. The leaves on the trees started to bud, but then it suddenly got cold again. A lot of trees were hurt.

4. Very cold weather can damage some plants. So, my mom and I always try to cover up our plants when we know the temperature is going to be below freezing.

5. We were able to save all of our plants last year by doing that. This year, we thought we would be successful. But then, one night there was an ice storm that we didn't expect. A lot of plants died.

PAGE 111
Answers will vary.
Sample answers:
I am trying hard to learn to juggle. I saw some jugglers at a street fair last year. That got me interested in juggling, so I got a book at the library. The book makes juggling sound easy, but it is not! First, you need to learn to catch and throw two balls with one hand. It's tricky. I practiced every day for two weeks. Finally, I could toss and catch perfectly with one hand. Then it was time to add the third ball. What a disaster! I will have to keep practicing.

PAGE 113
Answers will vary.

PAGE 114
Answers will vary.
Sample answers:
1. NASCAR Cars at the Beginning of the 21st Century
2. Rock and Roll Bands of the 1990's
3. The Gulf Stream
4. Care and Feeding of Horses
5. Geosynchronous Satellite Orbits—Why They're Useful

PAGE 116
Answers will vary.
Sample answers:
Edison's inventions:
transmitter, receiver for telegraph
telephone transmitter
phonograph (1st sound recording)
light bulb—1879
electric railroad
over 1,000 patents

PAGE 117
Answers will vary.
Sample answers:
II.B. phonograph
II.C. lightbulb
III. Thomas Edison's Other Interests
III.A. rubber substitutes
III.C. new uses for cement

PAGE 118
1. Under the Pacific Moon
2. Eric Gillen
3. Gregory and Clementine
4. exciting
5. likes oceans and adventure

PAGE 119
Answers will vary.

PAGE 120
1. Not all prehistoric animals were dinosaurs. For example, wooly mammoths were huge mammals. I wish they were still alive today. They're cool. Some prehistoric animals were closely related to the dinosaurs, like the pterosaurs. I once saw their bones in a museum. Other animals, such as the shark and the giant turtle, lived at the same time some dinosaurs existed, but neither of these water animals are dinosaurs. I once had a pet turtle.

2. Santa Rosa Island, now called Pensacola Beach, Florida, is famous for being the first place where shots were fired in the Civil War. It happened on the evening of January 13, 1861, when the Confederate army commanded the Union army to give up control of Fort Pickens. My family visited the site last summer. The Union refused, and the first shot was fired outside

the walls of Fort Pickens. The United States war sloop, Wyandotte, was anchored off the island. Florida has many small islands. 8,000 Confederate troops quickly moved into Pensacola, but they were not able to take Fort Pickens. Today Pensacola is a big town.

PAGE 121
Answers will vary.

PAGE 122
Answers will vary.

PAGE 123
Answers will vary.

PAGE 124
Acoustic Only: hollow body, strumming is loud
Both: six or twelve strings, long neck and body, pegs at the top of the neck, strum or pluck
Electric Only: solid body, holes for wires to amplifier, strumming is soft until plugged into amplifier

PAGE 125
Answers will vary.
Lions Only: tan
Both: large, belong to cat family, carnivores, expert hunters
Tigers Only: orange and black stripes

PAGE 126
Answers will vary.

PAGE 127
Answers will vary.
Sample answers:
One day my dad brought home a scraggly little bush in a pot. He said, "It's a rose bush."
"I don't believe it!" I said. "There aren't any roses on it!"
"Wait until spring. Then you'll see," he said.
I inquired, "Where did you get it?"
He said, "I found it on the curb. Someone was throwing it out."
"I'm not surprised they were throwing it away. It's ugly!" I said.
He just told me to "Grab a shovel and dig a hole."
So I did.
And wouldn't you know, this spring we had lovely roses in our yard!

PAGE 128
Answers will vary.

PAGE 129
Answers will vary.
Sample answers:
Look: mossy, hollow, tiny, black, marching to and fro, oozes, dried crystals
Feel: soft, sticky
Smell: pine, sharp, piney
Taste: sweet
Sound: peaceful, chattering, screeching

PAGE 130
Answers will vary.

PAGE 131
Answers will vary.

PAGE 132
Answers will vary.

PAGE 133
Answers will vary.

PAGE 134
Answers will vary.

PAGE 135
Answers will vary.
Sample answers:
Electric guitars and acoustic guitars have both similarities and differences. The numbers of strings they can have and their overall shapes are similar. They are played in a similar manner. However, the details of their construction are different, and an electric guitar can be much louder than an acoustic guitar when it is plugged into its amplifier.

PAGE 136
Answers will vary.
Sample answers:
Dear Alyssa,
How would you like a visitor? My mother has a business meeting in Chicago next month, and said I can join her for the week. If your parents say it's OK, I can hang out with you during the day while my mom is at her meetings. Wouldn't that be great?

I was in Chicago once when I was a baby. I do not remember anything about the trip. I'm excited to see the city again! My mom says Chicago is a fun city. We can go to a museum or just hang out and play. Let me know what your parents say. I can't wait to see you!
Love,
Marisol